The Way to Love Your Wife

Creating Greater Love and Passion
in the Bedroom

THE WAY TO
LOVE
YOUR
WIFE

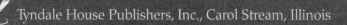

Tyndale House Publishers, Inc., Carol Stream, Illinois

CREATING GREATER
LOVE AND PASSION
IN THE
BEDROOM

Clifford L. Penner, Ph.D.
and Joyce J. Penner, M.N., R.N.

A Focus on the Family book published by
Tyndale House Publishers, Inc., Carol Stream, Illinois 60188

TYNDALE and Tyndale's quill logo are registered trademarks of Tyndale House
Publishers, Inc.

Portions of this book were originally published as *Men and Sex* © 1997 and *The
Married Guy's Guide to Great Sex,* © 2004 by Dr. Clifford Penner and Joyce Penner.

Library of Congress Cataloging-in-Publication Data
Penner, Clifford.
    The way to love your wife : creating greater love and passion in the bedroom / Clifford L.
Penner and Joyce J. Penner.
        p. cm.
    Includes bibliographical references.
    ISBN-13: 978-1-58997-445-6
    ISBN-10: 1-58997-445-X
    1. Husbands—Religious life. 2. Marriage—Religious aspects—Christianity. 3. Intimacy
(Psychology)—Religious aspects—Christianity. 4. Husbands—Sexual behavior. I. Penner,
Joyce. II. Title.
    BV4528.3.P46 2007
    248.8'425—dc22

                                    2006026134

Printed in the United States of America
2 3 4 5 6 7 8 9 / 13 12 11 10 09 08 07

To the men in our lives—

Our clients who have trusted us with the inner workings of their sexuality

And their wives who have informed us of the importance
of the husband's role in their sex lives

Our dear friend Dr. Neil Warren, whose enthusiasm has encouraged
and skill helped formulate the essence of this book

Our sons, Greg Penner and John Stellato, whose openness
and candor have kept us in touch with today's men

Our friends—
Peb Jackson for his active demonstration of his vision
and ministry with men of all ages

Jack Mount for his model of the servant leader to his family,
friends, and community

Paul Schultheis for his support in calling us to the meaning
of intimacy with God

Roland Hinz for his sincerity in his own life
and with us in seeking the truth

Bud Bare for his love and levity, which have lightened tense moments

Our brothers—Dave, Gene, and Doug Buhler for giving of themselves
to Joyce in teaching her loving relationships with men

Eldin Dirks and Jim Martens for bringing maleness
into Cliff's female-dominated family

— CONTENTS —

Preface ix
Introduction 1

1. This Isn't the NCAA 5
2. Does Good Sex Just Happen? 11
3. Go Her Way 29
4. Your Rights: Are Hers Yours? 47
5. Sex Is Not a Spectator Sport 55
6. Sex: A Path to Intimacy 65
7. When Sex Isn't Working 77
8. Affair Proof Your Marriage. 105
9. Have an Adventure with Your Wife 117
10. The Working Side of Sex. 125
11. The Lighter Side of Sex 137
12. Sex and Your Senses. 147
13. Pornography and the Internet 155
14. A Word to the Wives Is Sufficient 169

Notes 189
About the Authors 193

Is mutual sexual satisfaction really possible for every couple? Yes—and you as a man can make the difference!

Invest in discovering greater love, passion, and intimacy in your marriage, and your sex life will soar. Your gains will far exceed your efforts.

God designed sex to be a vital, passionate expression of marriage. During the early centuries of the church's growth, sex was a passion to be suppressed. When the sexual revolution of the 1960s and 1970s attempted to liberate people, it ended up degrading God's design.

Today, movements to build the family and to empower men to be men of God are being led by organizations such as Focus on the Family and Promise Keepers. We hope you'll make an additional promise: Commit yourself to read *The Way to Love Your Wife*—and to discovering greater love, passion, and intimacy with your wife.

Thank you and blessings,
DR. CLIFFORD AND JOYCE PENNER

Coming from German Mennonite homes and communities in the Midwest and Canada, we were sexually uninformed and naive. The only instruction either of us received from our families came to Joyce two weeks before the wedding. It was basically three warnings:

1. The honeymoon would be awful.
2. She would be very tired.
3. She shouldn't let him use her. (She didn't! She used him.)

Fortunately, Joyce had just taken a "preparation for marriage" class at her Baptist nursing school. The topic of sexual adjustment was a significant part of that class. So Joyce was the one who told Cliff what she'd learned about sex in marriage from a Christian perspective.

That's not how it's supposed to happen, of course. When it comes to sex, the man has to be the expert.

At least that's what they'd *like* you to believe.

The Making of a "Manly" Man

The false assumption that men are supposed to be the sexual experts has been passed from generation to generation.

Maybe it started for you around age five, when you were reprimanded for trying to peek into your sister's bedroom. You heard, "You're not supposed to do that." But you also heard "Boys will be boys," perhaps said with a tinge of pride.

In second grade you tried out sexual slang you'd heard from older guys. The adults frowned, but someone said, "He's practicing being a man."

In fifth grade, when the girls were sent to another room to

learn about menstruation, you were curious and felt left out. How dare they know about something sexual that was a mystery to you!

The subtle training of your expected manly expertise continued. Your cousin, two years older, showed you his stash of magazines. It was the first time you'd seen naked women, and it triggered an avalanche of fear and excitement and confusion. Those pictures made your gut churn as it had never churned before; you couldn't seem to breathe even though you were breathing fast, and the lump in your throat almost made you choke. You didn't want to look, yet couldn't get enough.

In middle school, real sex education started. You watched "the movie." The teacher talked about reproduction—how eggs unite with sperm and how babies are born. *Gross!* You could hardly listen. If you were in a class with boys only, you wondered what the girls were talking about. If you were in a mixed group, you couldn't keep from giggling when the teacher used a word like *penis, vagina,* or *intercourse.*

Either way, you tried to be cool—pretending you already knew all about that sex stuff. Being in the know sexually was cool for guys. The most popular boy in your class seemed to know the most about sex, always having a story about a girl or a sexual joke to tell.

The jokes seemed to tell you a lot about male sexual expertise and what it means to be a man. They implied that the real man is the one with the biggest penis—women are putty in his hands, and they beg for more.

Then it happened: The girls all grew up during that summer between middle school and high school. You were self-conscious all the time, trying to be what you knew you weren't. You got used to acting like a cool guy—or you backed away from girls to avoid the pain of rejection.

Whichever road you traveled, you had something in common with every other guy—masturbation. Maybe for you it just felt good. Or it only felt good until it was over and the flood of shame and guilt hit, and you vowed you'd never do that again. Perhaps peers had taught you that anyone who masturbates is a loser; masturbation was a sign that you couldn't get the real thing—a woman.

Through it all, you kept getting the message: Men are sexual experts and sexual animals. "Go for as much as you can get!" said your friends and the TV shows and the Internet porn sites. "The further you get, the more of a man you are." Even if you were raised with the biblical instruction to save intercourse for marriage, you may have pushed for as much as you could get. You counted on the girl to slam on the brakes. Sometimes you hoped she would; other times you hoped she wouldn't.

After high school, you wanted to be the sexual man the world expected you to be—even as your faith and church may have called you to save yourself for your wife.

Eventually you connected with the woman of your dreams. She may have been your first serious girlfriend or your tenth. When you got married, she may have expected you to be the sexual expert, too.

But were you? If you continued to function as though only you knew best, you probably encountered problems. She may even have lost interest in sex altogether.

It's not easy being the expert, is it?

Worse, it doesn't work.

Can You Take Direction?

Fortunately, there's another way.

Your sexual life can be wonderfully satisfying when you listen to your wife, honor her, and serve her by taking your cues from her. The servant leader finds he has the most responsive wife and the most passionate sexual life.

The fact is, *the only possibility for a life of sexual happiness occurs when the man moves in the direction of the woman.*

That means letting go of the false teachings of your early years. It means connecting with your wife, because of how she was created and how she was trained to nurture, touch, care, and feel. When you listen, respond, and let the woman lead, it's amazing how fulfilling sex is for both of you.

This book is about discovering greater love, passion, and intimacy in married sex by breaking down the myths about men and sex. *The Way to Love Your Wife* will empower you to make the difference in your sex life with your wife, whether it needs major repair or just a little improvement.

A lot of men find it tough to take directions even when they're lost. How much more difficult to take directions from your wife about sex! Yet sex works better when the man lets the woman set the pace. Solomon, a model of the sexually satisfied man, let his bride lead their physical relationship—as you'll see in this book. And Christ, the model of unselfish love, gave up His rights for His bride, the church.

A vibrant sexual relationship requires work, but that work leads to a lot more fun and a lifetime of passion. That's what *The Way to Love Your Wife* is all about.

After more than 25 years of being sexual therapists and leading sex seminars throughout the United States and Canada, we're convinced that understanding what works best in the bedroom won't just slightly improve your marriage.

We think it'll make you dizzy with exhilaration.

CHAPTER ONE

THIS ISN'T THE NCAA

Georgetown and UCLA are in the college basketball finals. The players are hyped, the coaches are hopeful and anxious. You, having put your dibs on Georgetown, have planned your day around the event.

Every time Georgetown scores, you're off the sofa with excitement. The tension builds. The fourth quarter ends with a tie, and the battle moves into overtime. Then a second overtime. Finally Georgetown scores, the buzzer sounds, the game is over, and your team is the winner.

You are a winner—*your* team won!

That night you get into bed with your wife, and you want to be a winner again.

In other words, you try to score.

Your wife's sexual responses are the baskets you make. The faster and more often you get a response, the more your excitement builds. You go for the hot spots—you manipulate and maneuver in order to gain points.

If there's no response, you get tense, frustrated. You're playing by the rules, aren't you? It doesn't seem fair. As soon as you figure out the rules, she changes them!

The harder you try, the worse things get. You're desperate. After all, if you were a real man, you could bring your wife to orgasm, more than one orgasm. If you can't, she's a loser—and so are you.

SEXUAL COMPETITIVENESS IN THE MAKING

Early Input

When did this game of winning and losing at sex really start?

Your father may have been filled with pride when, at 21 months, you could catch the green sponge football or tap the keys on his computer. "He seems so coordinated," Dad said, or, "He's exceptionally bright!" Someday, he secretly hoped, you'd make the family proud by tackling for the NFL or developing the next "killer app" software.

A few years later it was T-ball, soccer, or using your own computer. You heard Daddy tell Grandpa on the telephone about your catch, your two runs, or your amazing skill at chess. The message was coming through loud and clear: To feel good about yourself, you have to score, hit, catch, run, block, and rush. You have to win!

Most girls, meanwhile, were spending their early years differently. While most boys were playing a competitive game or wishing they were, girls pursued less competitive, more process-oriented activities like dance or music. Some girls were active in sports, but tended to talk while they played—making it less of a battle and more of a social event.

Maybe you weren't into sports, either—and your parents weren't obsessed with winning. Still, you probably saw the competition around you and either disdained it or measured yourself against it. Chances are those comparisons helped to form your self-image.

Puberty and Beyond

In middle school and high school, perhaps you continued to compete. Maybe you didn't go out for a team, but still went to games or saw them on TV. Whether you played or watched, the stakes were high. In everything from swimming to track to wrestling, the point was to score.

If you went to college, maybe you kept playing or watching. Or your interest may have shifted to other arenas—competing for the best grade in chemistry, the lead role in the play, the prettiest girlfriend, the winning vote in a student body election. In the working world you started to vie for the highest pay, the most impressive title.

> **Competing, achieving, arriving, scoring, hunting, and winning are natural inclinations for men.**

Competing, achieving, arriving, scoring, hunting, and winning are natural inclinations for men. It's no different when it comes to the sexual, romantic part of life.

IS SCORING WHAT IT'S ALL ABOUT?

We're amazed how often we hear this complaint from women: "It really bugs me when I'm cooking dinner or washing dishes and he comes and grabs me sexually."

What's that man trying to accomplish?

He's trying to be a winner. He thinks that to be a winner, he has to score; to score, he has to get her parts to respond.

That line of reasoning seems to start during dating. Guys ask each other questions like these:

"How far did you go?"

"How much did you get?"

"Did you get to third base?"

"Did you score?"

The assumption is that a man should push a woman as far as she will go. The further he can get her to go, the more of a winner he is.

Not true! Sex is not about achieving or scoring.

You Don't Win by Pushing for More

Before marriage, the man who pushes sexually puts the woman in the role of limit-setter. If you pushed to touch breasts or genitals, she had to draw the line. If you crossed it, you taught her to resist. Even if arousal allowed her to go along, she may have experienced sadness and pain afterward. She felt she'd given in to you.

> Sex is not about conquering, achieving, or scoring; sex is about relating.

A man who pushed for more before marriage is likely to continue the same approach after the wedding. He pushes for as much as he can get, yet senses that he isn't getting what really satisfies.

The goal-oriented approach won't lead to greater love, passion, or intimacy. Sex is about relating—not about conquering, achieving, or scoring.

Ultimately, goal-oriented sex doesn't score anyway. It doesn't even get you to first base. True gratification doesn't come from how fast or how often you get your wife to agree, to get aroused, to get you aroused, to reach an orgasm, or to have more than one orgasm.

That kind of sex leaves one or both lovers disappointed. For example, when you grab your wife's sexual parts because that feels good to you or you hope to get her interested in sex, she'll be turned off. In contrast, the woman who's attended and listened to, who feels cherished and adored, who's affirmed and pleasured will invite more touching and more intensity.

IT'S NOT WHETHER YOU WIN OR LOSE; IT'S HOW YOU PLAY THE GAME

Love, passion, and intimacy are never about winning or losing; they're about how you play the game. In sex, you need to go for the Mr. Congeniality Award rather than the Most Valuable Player.

Great sex requires a total shift in attitude from your natural instincts. A woman doesn't want to be a conquest or a win chalked up. Since the man is never truly satisfied unless the woman is, he has to move from his results-oriented approach to the process orientation of the woman. He has to learn to soak in the beautiful movements and harmony of the symphony instead of going for the winning of his team.

> Love, passion, and intimacy are not about winning or losing; they're about how you play the game.

That shift isn't easy. "It is natural for us to want to show affection.

But for some mysterious reason, we equate tenderness with senti-mentality, weakness and vulnerability. We seem to be as fearful to give as to receive it," wrote Leo Buscaglia.[1]

No wonder it's such a struggle for a man to feel good about himself in his relationship with his wife and in his relationship with God. Men want to win, but relationships require a completely dif-ferent approach.

You don't have to be a slave to the drive to score. You don't have to suffer the pressure, demands, and self-consciousness that results-oriented sex brings. You don't have to detach yourself from the good feelings of the moment.

In our practice of sexual therapy, we find that as couples learn to focus on the process of pleasure—rather than on the results of stimulation—they feel less demand. They're not merely satisfied; they're deeply fulfilled.

That's why, in the chapters that follow, we emphasize a focus on pleasure rather than on stimulation. If you want to have a mutually ecstatic sexual experience, you won't be trying to have one. You'll be attending to mutual pleasure.

To find out how that can happen in your marriage, read on.

CHAPTER TWO

DOES GOOD SEX JUST HAPPEN?

There it was in *U.S. News & World Report*: "Sexual Desire: Whether it's dull appetite or ravenous hunger, millions of Americans are unhappy with their intimate lives."

Good sex doesn't seem to be happening a whole lot in America today.

Perhaps it's partly because of our complex, busy lifestyles. But we think it's also because so many people mistakenly believe that good sex just happens.

Maybe good sex did just happen when Uncle Pete and Aunt Audrey lived on the farm without electricity and with no telephone and the house was dark and children were all snug in their beds by 7:00 P.M.

Then again, maybe not.

DOING WHAT COMES NATURALLY

We once gave an engaged couple a copy of our book *Getting Your Sex Life Off to a Great Start*. The bride-to-be thanked us and said,

"We won't read it until later, because we want to just do what comes naturally."

That young woman and her fiancé were in the top 1 percent of the nation in intelligence and education. They were spending time, energy, and money on wedding preparations, financial plans, and every other aspect of joining their lives together. But they didn't want to "ruin" their sex lives by preparing for the complex joining of their bodies, souls, and spirits.

They remind us of Joyce's 87-year-old grandmother, who told us years ago: "I don't agree with what you are doing [referring to us as sex educators]. Adam and Eve didn't need it, Abe and I didn't need it, and neither does anyone else."

> Sex doesn't just happen; you make sex happen.

The belief that good sex just happens—that you don't need to take responsibility for the quality of your sex life—is a myth perpetuated by many TV shows and movies. Men and women, usually unmarried, find themselves attracted irresistibly to each other; within minutes, it seems, they're having passionate, erotic sex. It all just happens.

Most couples want to have that kind of gut-grabbing sex. For some, it does just happen. But for the majority, a lifetime of exhilarating, fulfilling, and nurturing sexual experiences will take deliberate action.

Except in cases of rape, incest, and abuse, responsibility rests with each person for the quality and quantity of sex. When you falsely believe that sex happens to you rather than that you make sex happen, you'll tend to let sex within marriage slide into the doldrums. If you think sex is the automatic consequence of passion, you can proclaim innocence despite sexual behavior outside marriage. And if you're convinced that good sex just happens, you may believe you're no longer in love when it doesn't.

Many people equate being in love and sexual passion. They have a hard time telling the difference between eternal agape love and temporary, erotic love. Dr. Lewis B. Smedes, in *Love Within Limits*, explained the distinction:

> Eros flickers and fades as the winds of desire rise and wane. . . . If eros keeps waning it will eventually die. When the loved one no longer wills to meet the lover's needs, eros dies slowly. When the loved one leaves and does not come back, eros dies for lack of stimulation. When the lover has no more need of what the loved one wills to give, eros dies. Nourished by needs within the lover and the promise offered by the loved one, erotic love has no self-generating power. It is powerful, but it is not a power in itself.[1]

His bottom line: Both partners must will to keep sexual love alive in a marriage. Generally speaking, it doesn't just happen.

What Have We Done?

As for the two of us, we're blessed that our sex life has been delightful and natural from the start. We believe that's because of our similar backgrounds and the preparation for marriage class that Joyce took before our wedding.

In a sense, though, we didn't just do what came naturally. We applied what Joyce had learned in that class. And her eagerness to share that information with Cliff opened our communication about this vital dimension of our relationship.

We came from warm, nurturing homes that promoted a hard-work ethic and the value of setting and attaining goals. We saw marital and sexual happiness as a goal we could strive for and attain. That, we think, has allowed sex to flow as naturally for us as it has.

If you and your wife came to marriage as secure and confident individuals with healthy views of sexuality, realistic expectations, and adequate sexual knowledge, you may naturally share intense sexual gratification without much effort. You're uniquely blessed; healthy couples can have healthy sex by doing what comes naturally.

For many of us, though, it's not that simple.

WHEN NATURAL ISN'T NATURAL

The Sexually Naive Male

We've written in several of our books about the sexually naive man. Because he was raised in an overprotective home, or for other reasons, he missed some steps in his sexual development. He comes to marriage not knowing how to express his sexuality naturally.

What went wrong for this man? To understand that, we need to know what healthy sexual development looks like.

During the genitally focused two- to four-year-old stage of development, a boy discovers his penis and realizes that fondling it feels good. If he's shamed or restricted, his curiosity will be stifled; he won't learn that his genitals are a natural, pleasure-producing gift God gave him. On the other hand, if he's taught that his penis was designed by God with special feelings that are private and an important part of being a husband someday, he'll probably have a healthy attitude toward this part of his body.

As the boy moves into the preschool years, his curiosity takes the form of questions about sexuality. If he's affirmed for asking and given accurate information, he'll move on to school-age exploratory play. At this stage he wants to discover whether other boys are made the same as he is, and how girls are different. If he's taught boundaries and given information through books and talks rather than "field" experience, he'll learn respect and acceptance of his sexual awareness.

Then comes preadolescence, the middle school years, full of hormonal energy. The boy notices girls' development, may be aroused by it, and perhaps behaves inappropriately. We sometimes refer to this as the poke-and-run or kiss-and-run stage. Supervised group activities like passing oranges without using hands are good ways to help the preadolescent boy move into the adolescent dating years with confidence. Unfortunately, such innocent games are but a faint memory for many segments of society.

For the sexually naive man, this developmental process was interrupted at some point. He didn't enter adolescence with confidence. He comes to marriage still behaving like the middle school oaf—poking, pinching, and grabbing are his "natural" way of sexually approaching his wife.

His natural is not natural at all. It's a turnoff to his wife. As she responds with irritation, his confidence wanes—and he becomes even less natural.

If this describes you, be encouraged. Chances are you'll respond well to the kind of training this book offers. With the help of your wife, some exercises, and information, confident sexual functioning is only steps away. With newfound competence, your natural will indeed be natural.

WHEN NATURALS DIFFER

Claudia came to marriage assuming all men really want is sex. She expected her husband, Robert, to be the sexual pursuer. But in Robert's family, his mother was the vibrant, aggressive one. His father was more laid-back, responding to the advances of Robert's mother.

Robert and Claudia's tension over sex started on the wedding night. She went to unpack her things and get ready in the bathroom, expecting his pursuit. He relaxed and turned on the TV, waiting for her to come to him when she was ready.

The result was that she felt unwanted. He, meanwhile, was baffled by her hurt and felt unjustly criticized when Claudia referred to the incident as proof that he didn't desire her sexually.

Chris, another new husband, eagerly looked forward to his wedding night as the time to consummate his relationship with Angie. The two of them had been caressing, kissing, and fondling intensely during their engagement, impatient to move to intercourse. Chris assumed that he and Angie would pick up where they'd left off.

She, on the other hand, imagined they would start with the same level of involvement they'd experienced so far. When the night came, she lay on the bed of their elegant hotel room in her negligee, waiting for him to emerge from the bathroom. She pictured him coming out in nicely pressed pajamas.

When he opened the door, though, she was presented with his

nude body—including a full erection. Having been raised naive and with negative messages from her mother about male sexuality, she froze. They were unable to consummate their marriage for months.

Your Eagerness Turns Her Off

Eric, a man we interviewed for our video series, *The Magic and Mystery of Sex*, described his marriage: "I was like a little boy in a candy shop. I just wanted sex all the time, and I couldn't understand why we couldn't do it all the time."

A man's sexual eagerness is often his way of seeking love. It may be difficult to understand why a wife wouldn't want the same thing, but she often will feel used rather than loved by his pursuit. His eagerness pushes her away.

Men are more likely to connect and experience love through sex; women are apt to want sex as the consequence of feeling loved and

> Men connect and feel loved through sex; women desire sex as the consequence of feeling loved and connected.

connected. Understanding this male-female difference is central to negotiating a pleasing sexual relationship.

A woman needs to feel desired, but she also needs room to experience her own desire. If you always ask before she gets a chance to do the asking, she may respond as an expression of love; but over time her sexual intensity will dwindle.

When you're tempted to ask or pursue, try affirming and connecting emotionally instead. Keep her hungry—not satiated, and not starving.

Your Interest in Her Validates Her

Remember Claudia, the new wife who thought her husband, Robert, wasn't interested in her? She grew distrustful, critical, and demanding. Her expectations for sexual intimacy had been shattered. She felt negated. Her intense reaction made him feel inadequate and pushed him away even more—which, of course, increased her feelings of being unvalued.

> A wife is validated by her husband's sexual interest if that is expressed through connection and affirmation rather than pursuit or expression of need.

Maureen, another interviewee for our video series, was concerned because her husband, Dan, wasn't initiating sex. She worried that he no longer found her attractive: "Maybe he thought I was fat or something." Yet she was beautiful and trim.

A wife is affirmed by her husband's sexual interest if it's expressed by connecting with her and delighting in her rather than by pursuing her body. When your wife feels honored, adored, and cared for by you, your physical interest will be further indications of your love.

Gary Smalley communicates this need in *Go the Distance: The Making of a Promise Keeper* by John Trent:

> Honor is at the heart of all loving relationships—with God, our spouse and kids, our boss and co-workers. To honor someone is to attach high value to that person. It's a decision we make regardless of our feelings. When we decide to honor someone, we're saying the person is extremely valuable and important to us.[2]

When you don't communicate how much you value your wife, when you express your sexual interest solely by focusing on your needs or her body, she'll feel used.

As John Gray writes, men are motivated by feeling needed; women are motivated by feeling cherished.[3] That's why men often try to initiate sex with their wives by expressing their needs; men think women, like they, are motivated by being needed.

That doesn't work. But you can get both your *and* her needs met—if you recognize your differences.

When She's Not Like You

She says: "All men ever want is sex! They have only one thing on their minds!"

You say: "Women are so fickle. They're always changing their minds."

She says: "He never listens!"

You say: "Talk, talk, talk . . ."

She says: "Why does he never remember what I tell him?"

You say: "All she wants to do is shaaaaaare!"

She says: "If he just touched me the way I asked him!"

You say: "She got turned on when I did that yesterday!"

She says: "All I want to know is that he cares."

You say: "All I want is peace."

You like the room cold; she likes the room warm. You want to get to bed quickly; she'd rather spend what seems like an hour preparing. You'd like her to be on time; she'd rather look gorgeous and be late to meet you.

You get aroused when she fondles your penis; she pushes your hand away when you come into the kitchen and grab her breast or stroke her. She'd love to sit on the couch and have an evening of just kissing; you think, *Why would she want to kiss and get all excited if she doesn't want to have sex?*

You'd like an eager wife; she'd like a nondemanding husband. The list could go on and on, because there are hormonal and functional sexual differences between men and women. Here are some of them:

1. *The effect of frequency.* The longer the time between sexual encounters, the more a man wants sex and the more quickly he moves toward arousal and release. The opposite is true for a woman. The longer it's been since she's had sex, the less she desires it and the more time and connection she needs to experience pleasure and response.

2. *Body involvement.* For women, sex is more a "total person" event than a genital focus. That's why women need to experience connection and love to feel sexual; men feel sexual when they're stimulated and aroused. The total body response for women also explains why they tend to vary more from one sexual experience to another and from one woman to another.

3. *Orgasmic response.* Women have the capacity—not the necessity—to respond with multiple or sequential orgasms. Most men, however, require a rest period after ejaculation before they can be restimulated to another erection. That may be 20 minutes or 20 hours. A woman's orgasm can be stopped at any point by internal barriers, fears, or external distractions; once a man starts his ejacula-

tory response, it can't be stopped. If he wishes to delay ejaculation, that control has to happen before he is about to ejaculate.

4. *Dysfunctions.* Men can experience difficulty with getting or maintaining erections or ejaculating too quickly; women can have orgasmic pressure and inhibition. This is probably because men in our culture tend to be more active during sex than do women, and arousal is controlled by the passive branch of the autonomic (involuntary) nervous system. Orgasm, meanwhile, is triggered when the active branch of the autonomic system goes into action.

5. *Readiness.* We agree for the most part with Barry McCarthy, author of *Male Sexual Awareness,* when he says in an interview with Paula M. Siegel that "men are by and large automatic functioners: They come to the sexual interaction already anticipating it, already aroused, and become frustrated if their partner isn't equally ready for intercourse. They measure their sexual satisfaction by quantity rather than quality. Women, needing some interaction to become aroused, are always playing catch-up with their partner. They tend to be much more concerned with the quality of their lovemaking than the quantity."[4]

The differences between men and women lead to the greatest conflict—and the most intense intrigue. We think of men as more predictable, easier to please, not as complicated, and more basic. We think of women as the new, improved model; after all, they were created after men.

Women are more complex, less predictable. A woman is like an ocean—ever-changing, multidimensional.

You might say, "Why didn't God make women more like men? It would be so much easier."

We say, "But how boring!"

And how impractical. For the combination of male constancy and ever-changing femininity is the key to keeping sex alive over a lifetime of being married to the same person.

> **The combination of male constancy and ever-changing, complex femininity is the key to keeping sex alive in marriage.**

With every discussion of male and female differences, of course, individuals will find they're the exceptions. Some women identify with generalizations about men, and vice versa. It's important that you and your wife learn about *your* differences.

As you do, make those differences work for you rather than against you. Understanding them is central to resolving sexual conflicts and opening avenues of passion in your marriage.

ALLOW SPACE TO BE NATURAL

Spontaneity is great if you're happy with the results—if it brings the love, passion, and intimacy you and your wife want. For some couples, it does.

For most, though, doing "what comes naturally" requires a little planning. Anticipating being together builds quality, and the allotment of time increases quantity.

Looking Forward to It

Remember planning some of your most exciting dates? What made them special?

Probably it was attention to detail—making the conditions right—and anticipating the event.

For a married couple, enjoying a lifetime of exhilarating and fulfilling sex requires preparation. A great sex life is based on more than just bringing two bodies together because each passionately desires the other. That may work in the movies and early in marriage, but it's based on the assumption that sex happens to you. The truth is that *you* are the ones who choose the quality and quantity of your sexual experiences.

Many couples fear they won't be "in the mood" if they plan for sex. But planning can prepare your mood. If you arrange the conditions necessary for both of you, the quality and intensity of your sexual times together will escalate.

Anticipation especially allows a woman to meet the conditions she needs for an intimate time with her husband. Plan to eliminate or at least reduce the possibility of interruptions that kill passion. Turn off the ringer on the telephone, put up a DO NOT RING DOORBELL sign, make sure the children are asleep or staying at a friend's house, feed and change the baby. (When our children were babies we were convinced they had automatic sensors and did not want us to have sex.) Wrap up tasks and thoughts that are likely to preoccupy you.

Anticipation also helps a woman get in touch with her body and her sexuality. Fantasizing about the upcoming event, taking a special oil bath, shaving her legs, remembering past erotic experiences with you, or exercising can spark a woman's sexual energy.

The Times of Your Sex Life

How often should you plan to be together? What kinds of togetherness should you anticipate? Here are six suggestions.

1. *Daily check-ins.* Couples who connect physically in some way every day will have sex more often and enjoy more pleasure

when they do. Daily connecting times can happen around leaving for work, coming home, after dinner, at bedtime, or whenever works best for the two of you. If daily physical contact isn't happening naturally, look together at your schedules and select a time to connect.

> **Couples who connect physically daily will have more frequent and more enjoyable sex.**

Daily connecting times might last five to fifteen minutes or more. Use them to share the content of each other's day, check on how your relationship is going, pray together, and read together.

And kiss. Celebrate your relationship with kisses. Kiss softly and tenderly, passionately and warmly. Kiss when you feel sad or happy. We see kissing as the barometer measuring a couple's intimacy and passion. Rarely have we had a couple seek sexual therapy who were still kissing regularly and passionately.

Ask your wife how she feels about your kissing. If either of you isn't happy with the other's kissing, take an evening to show and tell each other how you like to kiss. Take turns leading. Note that a good kisser is usually not too hard and not too tentative, not too wet and not too dry, lingers but not too long, and uses his tongue gently and playfully but not forcefully. Try seeing how many ways of kissing you know.

2. *Quickies.* We don't recommend five to seven minutes after the 11:00 news, but "quickies" are a snack that can keep most couples going until they have time for a more nutritious delight.

Although in general all sexual experiences must be mutually satisfying, quickies can be for one or the other or both of you. They can include intercourse, orgasm, or ejaculation, or none of the above. They never violate; they are engaged in only by mutual agreement. They may give more to one than the other, but they never take from one in a depleting sense.

A quickie can be fun—an afternoon delight, a sunrise special, or a bedtime snack. They can't be the mainstay of your sexual diet, though. You can survive on them, but you won't grow.

3. *Regular dinners.* We recommend that regular sexual times happen about once a week, or more or less depending on each person's needs. Plan these encounters to bring your worlds and bodies together, to pleasure and enjoy each other, to allow arousal, release, and intercourse as desired.

These "meals" should be satisfying for both spouses, occurring when neither is fatigued or rushed. Both should be active participants,

> **Time allotment formula for a successful marriage: fifteen minutes per day, one evening per week, one day per month, and one weekend per quarter.**

free to pursue their desires without violating the other, communicating verbally and nonverbally their likes and dislikes. Weekly "dining" with these conditions will help keep a relationship alive and thriving.

4. *Smorgasbord.* To add variety, try a time together in which you're free to ask for what you want. Each partner takes a turn choosing favorites from a list—written or not—of sexual activities. You might have a "his" night and a "hers" night. Or take turns being pleasurer and receiver.

5. *Nouvelle cuisine.* Many restaurants these days feature light, delicious fare creatively presented. The flavors are novel, the tastes

linger, and you finish the meal satisfied but not full. *Nouvelle* sex is much the same. It seeks not so much to satiate but to satisfy with newness, wonderful sensations, and visual enjoyment. Create your own excitement; try using ideas from the "Ten Ways to Have Fun with Sex" section in Chapter 11.

6. *Gourmet delights.* A diet of gourmet meals would be too rich, but being left with that overfed feeling is enjoyable every now and then. Occasionally take a whole day or weekend to fully appreciate each other. As with your other encounters, it should be mutually desired and enjoyable. You'll find it can be a wonderfully satiating experience.

Whatever the focus of your time, be sure to set it aside. Our guideline for your private relationship—romantic and physical— is fifteen minutes per day, one evening per week, one day per month, and one weekend per quarter. We suspect following that formula for time to connect and care will leave both of you happy and satisfied.

NEGOTIATE YOUR SEXUAL RELATIONSHIP

Sometimes good sex just doesn't take place naturally. Sometimes you want to discover greater love, passion, and intimacy in your marriage.

When that happens, set aside time to identify your differing needs. Negotiate a mutually satisfying sexual relationship. You may even want to do it in writing.

To begin, individually write out or say how you'd like your sexual relationship to be. Here are some questions to answer:

- How often would you like physical contact?
- What kind of contact should it be?

- Who would initiate it?
- What preparation would be important?
- What time of day is best?
- How long should your times last?
- What activities would be included?

Add anything else the two of you would like to include in your plan for sexual intimacy.

Negotiating a sexual relationship may seem like a cold approach. But you'll be surprised how much warmth can be sparked when two people feel their sexual needs are heard and respected and a plan for those needs is instituted.

You're different, you and your wife. It's unrealistic, at least in the long term, to expect that good sex will happen naturally without working out those differences.

Great sex in marriage requires much more than a natural response to passion. When the initial blaze of a new relationship cools a bit, the transition to a deeply fulfilling sexual life that will last for decades requires focusing on your relationship in general and your sex life specifically. That transition is most likely when you know yourselves and each other intimately, behave lovingly toward each other, are trustworthy and trusting—and anticipate and plan for your sexual times.

CHAPTER THREE

GO HER WAY

Joyce walked by Cliff's desk and said, "This is so much fun, writing together!" Working as a team vitalizes her. Not that Cliff doesn't benefit. But sharing, communicating, and feeling connected are basic to a woman's essence. In the process of uniting, she feels loved.

Every person needs to be loved by God and by others. Longing for intimacy with God and people is an effort to counteract our sense of loneliness.

When it comes to marriage, men may need connection as much as women do—but for most it's not a *felt* need. Men tend to want sex to meet their need for connection; women tend to go for intimacy because they need connection to want sex.

Since women feel the need for intimate union more directly, we recommend that you "go her way." You'll be happier, and sex will work best, when you move in the direction of your wife.

To do that, you'll need to understand some things about women in general—and your wife in particular.

KNOW YOUR WIFE

Cliff grew up with his mom, dad, and three sisters. He knew many of the ways in which women are different from men. Joyce grew up with her dad, mom, three brothers, and a sister. Her comfort with male-female differences was based on experience, too.

Whether or not you lived in a home with sisters, you'll have to know about women and how they differ from men. Here are seven areas that deserve your special attention.

> Since a man's need for connection is not felt like a woman's, we recommend you go her way.

1. *Nurturing Needs.* Only a woman can have a child grow inside her. God made women with the ability to physically and emotionally nurture a fetus and infant. He made them with hormones that promote nurturing tendencies. We believe that because of God's design, women crave nurturing more than men do.

When you accept the fact that your wife probably has a greater felt need for this emotional connection than you do, it frees you from trying to manufacture needs you don't have. It also frees you to respond to her need on her terms. Responding to her nurturing needs will bring greater sexual intimacy, too.

2. *Hormonal Patterns.* Hormonal differences between men and women start in the womb. The male hormone testosterone must kick in sufficiently to make a boy a boy, for example.

Estrogen and progesterone control many more functions in women than testosterone does in men. The female hormones trigger monthly emotional patterns and abilities such as breast-feeding. The more you understand female hormones and their effect on your wife, the more you'll be able to "go her way."

To help both of you gain that understanding, we recommend that a woman keep a special calendar. Items to include: the days of her menstrual cycle (if she's still menstruating), an indication of her mood, awareness of her needs, sexual interest, sexual activity and how that was for her, and other issues that affect you, her, or your relationship. It should be *her* private calendar, not your evaluation of her. To the degree that she's comfortable doing so, she can share the results of this record with you.

3. *Emotional and Relational Desires.* A woman needs to feel cared for; she needs to feel that her personhood is regarded and is more important to her husband than her body is. When she feels understood and affirmed, she yearns for sexual union with her husband.

> **Accept your wife's greater need for nurturing.**

Sorting out feelings is difficult for many men. How can you know what goes on inside your wife when you can't even figure out what goes on inside yourself—especially if it doesn't even seem important?

Start by deciding to get to know your wife emotionally and relationally and then consciously doing it. Practice is necessary. Listening and understanding may not be natural for you, but you'll be greatly rewarded. Your wife will respond enthusiastically, even if your attempts are faltering.

This may sound like a gimmick, but it isn't! There's no way you can fake it over the long haul, and she'd spot it anyway if you tried. When you genuinely attend to her, she'll feel loved—and more sexually open and interested.

4. *Domestic Needs.* Many women have no energy left for sex by the end of the day; it's been burned up by working at a job, keeping up the house, preparing meals, mothering children, and more. Even if you help, she'll feel burdened if she alone "owns" all these

duties. Take on some of her commitments; it'll lift a big load off her shoulders and free some energy to share with you.

Ask your wife what help would best serve her. Pay attention to her feelings of pressure and stress, and communicate yours. Negotiate a system of caring for each other that respects each person's needs. She'll receive your concern as an important expression of your love.

> **Men go for the short-term solution of sex to feel loved and connected; women yearn for sexual union when their personhood is regarded.**

5. *Spirituality.* Find out what's important for your wife to feel spiritually connected with you. Take leadership in your spiritual relationship if that works for her. If she's the one who thinks more about reading the Bible and praying together, support her as she makes suggestions. On the other hand, if she feels pressured by you spiritually, back off. Ask her where she would like to begin.

Frequently women express frustration over the lack of spiritual connection between themselves and their husbands by saying, "All he ever wants is sex!" Instead, negotiate ways to meet your separate needs for spiritual intimacy.

6. *Sexual Conditions.* All of us have conditions that are necessary for us to give ourselves sexually. Dr. Archibald Hart reported in his book *The Sexual Man* that not waiting for the right conditions for sex is the main cause of marital sexual problems.[1]

Most people, though, haven't thought about or defined the conditions. The two of you might enjoy doing that with each other. Conditions may include timing, state of restedness, cleanliness, who initiates, privacy, and much more. Defining conditions will reduce stress and guessing.

She, being a woman, may have more requirements than you do. That may bother you. Men often ask us, "Why can't we just *do* it? By the time we meet all her conditions, I don't even *want* to do it."

When the conditions themselves become a demand, they need to be negotiated. The person needing the conditions must take more responsibility for them. When each person's conditions are negotiated and respected, attended to, and then moved past, sex can reach its maximum potential.

> When you genuinely attend to your wife, her heart will open to you, and her sexual attraction to you will increase.

7. *Sexual Triggers.* A man often gets "triggered" by seeing his wife in the nude, undressing, or wearing something provocative. Some women "get in the mood" by seeing their husbands in these ways, but not usually.

A look, a touch, a compliment, a kiss given rather than requested, availability without demands, time together, conversation, and pampering—these are more likely sexual triggers for women.

Your wife may know what triggers her sexually. She may never have thought to tell you, or may believe that if you loved her, you would know. Revealing her secret could be a major change in your sexual relationship. Once you know this information, don't use it to get what you want; respect it to give her what she desires.

MOVE IN HER DIRECTION

Knowing your wife is only the beginning; you also need to move in her direction.

You start by "getting with her" as a person. This is an all-day, everyday process. It's not something you do at 10:40 P.M. so that you can have sex at 10:45.

It's a radical concept. You may not like the idea at first, but it works. It's also the key concept in this book.

If you remember nothing else, remember this: For the greatest pleasure and sexual satisfaction, learn to listen to and follow your wife's lead and respond to her desires.

Why does it work this way? Here are four reasons.

She's More Complex

Your wife is a very complicated creature—emotionally, hormonally, spiritually, relationally, and sexually. Her variety and intensity may appear in the sexual realm as unpredictability and strong reactions—both of which can intimidate and confuse you.

A woman's sexual complexity is seen in anatomy and in sexual response. Let's look at each of them.

Anatomically, the primary sex organ for the man is the penis; the woman's genitals—clitoris, labia, vagina, and other detailed parts—are her primary sex organ. The man has testicles, a prostate gland, and a tube that carries the sperm and seminal fluid to the outside of the body, but the woman's reproductive system is more involved. She has a uterus with ovaries that produce and release eggs as they mature, plus the upper and lower vaginal canal. The woman's urinary system is completely separate from her reproductive system.

> **Sexually, a woman has both more complex body parts and more complex bodily responses.**

A woman's sexual response happens on several fronts. She has many more body parts to enlist in the sexual experience than the man does—which partially explains why it takes her longer to get aroused. Externally, there are clitoral engorgement, changes in the inner and outer labia, and nipple erection. Internally, she experiences engorgement of the outer third of the vagina, ballooning of the inner two-thirds of the vagina, the pulling up and away of the uterus so that the penis doesn't strike it, and other internal organ responses. She also has two centers of orgasmic response—vaginal and uterine contractions.

She's More Comprehensive

For the woman, sex is a total-body and total-person experience. It's good for her when her husband attends to all of who she is, not just her sexual parts.

According to an Ann Landers survey, women reported that if they had to choose between cuddling and sexual intercourse, they'd choose cuddling.

Why? Perhaps it's because cuddling involves the whole body—and connects with the whole person.

She's More Internal

The male genitals are "right out there"; the female genitals are close to the body and covered or internal.

For a man, much of the sexual experience is external. The more aroused he gets, the farther his penis may protrude. When he ejaculates, semen is expelled from his body.

For a woman, it's just the opposite. Though her arousal often begins with external stimulation, her response is mostly internal. Even the outward reactions of the clitoris and labia are hidden. As her arousal intensifies, the changes move inward. The deepest responses of orgasm—contractions of the uterus and vagina—are reported as pulsations that resonate from the very core of her being and ripple out in waves to encompass her whole body.

She Operates on Two Tracks

People often say that a man has a one-track mind. A woman has at least a two-track, if not a multitrack, mind.

When a man has an erection, it's natural for him to be ready for entry and eager to move to the culmination of the sexual experience. For a woman, physical arousal doesn't ensure readiness to proceed. She can lubricate vaginally and have nipple erection within 10 to 30 seconds of initial physical stimulation, yet be far from ready to proceed to intercourse or orgasm.

> For a woman, both physical arousal and emotional readiness are necessary for her to proceed to intercourse and orgasm.

In other words, her body may be physically prepared. But emotionally, she may not be receptive. She must experience an emotional meshing and blending and connecting with her husband before she can feel ready to open herself up to him—to take him inside her and be bound in that deep, one-flesh way.

This two-track system can be hard for a man to understand. But if you're going to be sensitive to your wife and serve her needs, you'll accept it. You'll allow her the time and the conditions for both tracks—the emotional connection and the physical responsiveness.

Moving in your wife's direction adds richness to your sexual experience. Conversely, trying to get in sync with you brings emptiness for her. Let her set the pace, and you'll both be ready to proceed with a sense of togetherness.

SHE LISTENS TO HER BODY; YOU LISTEN TO HER

Some would call King Solomon the greatest lover of all time. Reading the love poetry of the Song of Solomon, you'll find a model of how sex works best when a husband lets his wife set the speed limits.

Why Solomon Sang

Solomon talks adoringly about the wonderful attributes of his bride. He compliments her loveliness and lavishes every detail of her beauty with praise: "You are altogether beautiful, my darling, and there is no blemish in you" (Song of Solomon 4:7).

He adores her hair, cheekbones, lips, eyes, and belly. He uses symbolic language to describe his enjoyment of her sexual parts. He delights in every aspect of her personhood and her sexuality.

What does this do for her? It ignites her passion. She wants him closer, inviting him to taste the sexual fruits of her body:

Awake, O north wind,
And come, wind of the south;
Make my garden breathe out fragrance,
Let its spices be wafted abroad.
May my beloved come into his garden
And eat its choice fruits! (Song of Solomon 4:16)

She invites at her pace and asks for the degree of physical involvement she would like. He responds to her invitation:

I have come into my garden, my sister, my bride;
I have gathered my myrrh along with my balsam.
I have eaten my honeycomb and my honey;
I have drunk my wine and my milk (Song of Solomon 5:1).

Whew!

The Formula

Here's how it worked for Solomon, and how it can work for you:

1. The husband adores his wife.

2. As she feels adored, her passion is ignited and she invites him sexually.

This is another core concept, the key to a lasting, fulfilling sexual life.

Think back on your courting days. You probably were full of praise for your bride-to-be, and she responded. Her desire for you made you feel great, so you expressed even more positive feelings for her. In turn, she became hungry for more. Within the boundaries the two of you set, her responsiveness and interest left you deeply satisfied.

> The Formula:
> The husband adores his wife; his affirmation ignites her passion, and she invites him sexually.

This positive feedback system doesn't have to stop when you get married. It can continue throughout life. As you adore her and she invites you, mutual affirmation will flow.

We talked once with a man who had a national ministry. He was good at sensing the pulse of a church and helping it move to greater depth and insight.

Yet his wife felt lonely, left out, unheard. Because of his inattentiveness, she was rarely interested in sex. They hadn't had sex in about six months.

We suggested that he practice with her what he did with congregations—sensing what she might be experiencing and communicating that to her. Hesitantly he took steps toward that kind of empathy, and within three days she was inviting him to be with her sexually.

Why? Because she felt his attempt to hear and connect with her.

Every woman needs to know that her husband is genuinely interested in her, her life, and her feelings. Feeling cared about is far better than getting flowers or chocolates. Then sexual interest follows.

Free Her to Take

Your adoration will build your wife's confidence in her own sexuality. That, in turn, helps her to receive.

For the sexual experience to be good for both spouses, the woman has to be free to take—to take in touch, pleasure, arousal, and passion. Then she can go after what she needs. When she gets it—not by demand but by invitation—she's happy, and so are you. No one loses! It's a win-win situation.

> You both win when she learns to listen to her body and go after what she needs.

If your wife has difficulty receiving, you may wish for a "take" switch to turn on inside her body. Like it or not, that switch is inside her brain.

If she believes her duty is to give to you and please you rather than to take, she'll need help to be in the experience for her pleasure. Making that shift will take time; think of this as a long-term goal. Over the next two years the two of you can work on helping her to be oriented toward her own fulfillment rather than aiming to please you. You'll be pleased with the results!

> **KEY CONCEPT:**
> Keep your pace lagging behind your wife's pace in both sexual activity and intensity.

Setting the Pace

The Song of Solomon describes the bride leading the sexual experience. She says in 5:3, "I have taken off my dress, . . . I have washed my feet." She prepares her body, searches for him, and invites his fondling and entry into her body. Aroused by his adoration of her, she describes her vaginal lubrication (fingers dripping with liquid myrrh) and her body opening up to him.

In our marriage seminars, virtually every woman nods enthusiastically when we talk about the need for the man to slow down. As a popular song once emphasized, every woman loves a man with a "slow hand."

Sexually speaking, men usually move faster than women. But the man should keep his pace behind that of his wife, both in intensity and in activity. One couple compared this to riding bikes together, with the husband always keeping his front wheel just behind the wife's.

The need for the woman to set the pace and guide the touch is crucial when it comes to clitoral stimulation. Most men are too direct. Women generally prefer a light, whispery touch—not on the head of the clitoris but on the hood, stroking the pubic hair, or on the shaft, stroking the inner lips.

The type of touch a woman desires can change from day to day or even moment to moment, so your wife needs to teach and guide you. The more you're aroused, the more likely you'll forget and touch her with the speed and intensity you prefer. If you lag behind her and let her guide you, your tendency to speed up will be checked.

To do this, your wife must feel free to listen to her needs and pass them on to you. Encourage her to communicate in words as well as nonverbal signals. You might start by having her teach you how to pleasure her with the kind of touch and at the pace she likes. She can guide you by moving her body or your hands. As you become more secure, you'll take this not as criticism but as proof that she feels free to pursue pleasure. With time, she'll probably need to guide you less often.

Here are two exercises you can try. In both cases, sit with your back against the head of the bed; she sits between your legs with her back to your chest.

In the first one, she teaches you by placing her hands over yours and using your hands to pleasure the front of her body. In the second, she talks constantly as you pleasure her; she's giving you a play-by-play account of what she's feeling and thinking.

You can reverse roles and teach her about yourself, too. Create your own versions of these learning tools. Once you've tackled the awkwardness of communicating openly about your sexual likes and dislikes, she'll find it much easier to ask for and go after what she needs during your sexual times.

Touchy Subjects

Speed isn't the only issue when it comes to touching your wife in the way she prefers. Here are four more things to keep in mind:

1. *Touch in circles.* Men tend to touch in straight lines. But women generally like to be touched in circular motions.

> **Men tend to touch in straight lines; women like to be touched in circular motions.**

It's a little like their communication styles. Men tend to cut to the chase; women tend to circle toward their main point.

When Joyce is telling Cliff about an event, a purchase, or a feeling, Cliff usually says, "Just give me the bottom line." That bugs Joyce; she likes to tell everything that *leads up to* and *explains* the bottom line. She circles in to make her point rather than going straight for it.

Dr. John Gray noted this difference between men and women:

> Women enjoy conversation most when they are not required to get to the point right away. Many times, to relax or to get closer to someone, they like to circle around for a while and gradually discover what they want to say. This is a perfect metaphor for how a woman enjoys sex. She loves it when a man takes time to get to the point and circles around for a while.[2]

When you touch your wife, try a circular motion. Go with her bodily design. Encourage her to invite circular touching when you revert to straight stroking.

2. *Limit same-spot touching.* Don't wear it out! A guy tends to

stay in one place too long. He finds a spot that works and then rubs it until it's numb.

Keep your wife hungry for more; don't make her want to push you away. It's much better to leave when she wants more than to stay until she wishes you weren't there.

3. *Count on change.* A touch that worked last time may not work this time. Such unpredictability is a common frustration for men; they want to figure things out, find the answer. Tension can bubble up when your wife recoils from a caress that once produced a positive response.

> **You can never know whether what worked last time will work this time.**

Accept this as an ingredient that makes your sexual life interesting. A woman's fluctuations keep things lively. Her changeableness is another reason why it's essential to follow her lead.

4. *Tease with promise.* Teasing touch has a place in the sexual experience, but it must be positive for both partners. It can't be at your or her expense or cause frustration.

Teasing touch makes the other person hungry, like smelling chocolate cookies baking in the oven. It causes anticipation. It's a promise!

Sexual tease pledges to fulfill; it doesn't withhold. It circles rather than going straight for the hot spots. It builds the intensity of the pleasure as you move toward erotic stimulation and then move away.

As you enjoy touching your wife's body and roam toward her nipples, clitoris, or vagina, don't quite go there. Get close, then circle back to more general bodily touching. As you approach the breasts and genitals again, do so with the lightest touch. Next time you stroke those areas, linger for a moment.

You might pause for ten seconds in the middle of thrusting, but not to frustrate her. If the pause occurs when her wave of arousal has peaked or dipped, it can heighten her hunger. A pause as she is climbing, however, can feel like withholding. The purpose of teasing touch is to allow her to invite more.

Remembering Her Needs

Women get frustrated with men because men don't remember. A wife can be convinced she's told her husband a hundred times exactly what she likes sexually, but he doesn't do what she asked. Yet he protests that he doesn't know what she wants.

Why? We think a man's memory is in inverse proportion to his arousal. A friend suggested that his blood is no longer in his brain. With arousal, the blood leaves his brain and goes where there *is* no memory!

There are two real reasons why wives believe their husbands should know what they like—and why husbands seem not to know.

First, husbands seem to have difficulty believing and remembering that wives' enjoyment of sex is so different from their own.

Second, wives seem to have a tough time taking responsibility for keeping their husbands informed of their sexual desires and needs. Believing the myth that men are the sexual experts, they fantasize that a truly loving husband will sweep her off her feet. He'll be the knight in shining armor who switches on her hunger for him. When that doesn't happen, she's disappointed that she has to tell him what she does and doesn't like.

Both of you can reverse your inclinations. You can recognize that what's natural for you may not be natural for her. She can realize that there's no way for you to know her whim in any given moment.

As you listen and she communicates her needs, you'll remember. She'll be happy, and intimacy will grow.

A Word of Warning

When we talk about following your wife's lead, we don't mean you should be passive or shut down your own sexuality. It's important that you continue to listen to yourself and express your desires with affirmation and without demand.

Your wife's leading doesn't give her permission to be uncaring about you. Her sensitivity in leading is just as important as your sensitivity in allowing her to lead. Her role is about setting the pace, learning to take, and pursuing her sexuality with you.

TO BE GREAT, SEX MUST BE GOOD FOR BOTH OF YOU

As you adore your wife, delight in her, talk to her, touch her, and move at her pace, she'll respond in ways that make sex better than you'd ever imagined.

Sex without that kind of intimacy is possible, of course. Sex with prostitutes or involving Internet images falls into that category. But sex that brings two people together in a deep, lifelong bond of love, passion, and joy is found only in marriage.

To be great, sex has to be as good for her as it is for you. That happens when you move in her direction.

If you doubt this, try it for a couple of months. You may be surprised.

CHAPTER FOUR

YOUR RIGHTS: ARE HERS YOURS?

S ome men think that when they marry, their wives' bodies become theirs to possess. Here's an extreme example from a *Los Angeles Times* article:

> When Ramiro Espinosa used a butter knife to unlock the door to his wife's attic bedroom two years ago and then demanded sex from her, he figured he had the Catholic Church on his side.
>
> But when he tried to use that as a defense last week against charges of attempted rape and spousal abuse, it didn't quite work. Catholic officials said he was wrong and a judge sentenced him to a year in County Jail.
>
> "People have been dragging religion into the bedroom for eons," say sexual therapists Clifford and Joyce Penner, who are sometimes known as "the Christian Masters and Johnson."
>
> "In the New Testament, the debate usually centers around a passage in the apostle Paul's first letter to the Corinthians:

'The husband and wife should fulfill their conjugal obligations toward each other. A wife's body does not belong to her alone, but also to her husband, and the husband's body to his wife. Do not deprive one another.' "[1]

GIVE HER YOURS; SHE GIVES YOU HERS

Those Scripture verses are instructions for living, to be personally applied. They're not to be used as justifications for judging or demanding. Some men use 1 Corinthians 7:3-5 to insist on their sexual rights—or instill guilt in their wives for not fulfilling their "wifely Christian duty."

Here's what the passage actually says:

> Let the husband fulfill his duty to his wife, and likewise also the wife to her husband. The wife does not have authority over her own body, but the husband does; and likewise also the husband does not have authority over his own body, but the wife does. Stop depriving one another, except by agreement for a time that you may devote yourselves to prayer, and come together again lest Satan tempt you because of your lack of self-control.

That's a guide for what *you* can do to make your sexual relationship better, not ammunition for a battle over what God wants your *spouse* to do.

The best way to sexual fulfillment is to realize that your body isn't just yours; it's also your wife's. Don't withhold yourselves; give yourselves freely to each other as Christ gave Himself for the church and wants the church to give itself to Him.

THE WAY TO LOVE YOUR WIFE

How can you love your wife as Christ loved the church? It sounds impossible. But the apostle Paul has these words of encouragement:

> Not that I have already obtained it, or have already become perfect, but I press on in order that I may lay hold of that for which also I was laid hold of by Christ Jesus. Brethren, I do not regard myself as having laid hold of it yet; but one thing I do: forgetting what lies behind and reaching forward to what lies ahead, I press on toward the goal for the prize of the upward call of God in Christ Jesus (Philippians 3:12-14).

You can't perfectly love your wife as Christ loved the church. But the goal gives you a standard to work toward.

Servant Headship

You're the head of your wife, as Christ is the head of the church. This concept of headship is laid out in Ephesians 5:22-27:

> Wives, be subject to your own husbands, as to the Lord. For the husband is the head of the wife, as Christ also is the head of the church, He Himself being the Savior of the body. But as the church is subject to Christ, so also the wives ought to be to their husbands in everything. Husbands, love your wives, just as Christ also loved the church and gave Himself up for her; that He might sanctify her, having cleansed her by the washing of water with the word, that He might present to Himself the church in all her glory, having no spot or wrinkle or any such thing; but that she should be holy and blameless.

Servant leadership includes characteristics Christ modeled:
1. He was ready to serve.
2. He didn't shy away from difficult challenges.
3. He gave up His rights for us.

Relinquish Your Rights

You have a right to sexual fulfillment with your wife; you're also commanded to love your wife as Christ loved the church. Christ's right was to remain with God the Father; He gave up that right for a time because of His love for the church:

> Do nothing from selfishness or empty conceit, but with humility of mind let each of you regard one another as more important than himself; do not merely look out for your own personal interests, but also for the interests of others. Have this attitude in yourselves which was also in Christ Jesus, who, although He existed in the form of God, did not regard equality with God a thing to be grasped, but emptied Himself, taking the form of a bond-servant, and being made in the likeness of men. And being found in appearance as a man, He humbled Himself by becoming obedient to the point of death, even death on a cross (Philippians 2:3-8).

Sometimes you may have to give up your right to sexual fulfillment in order to love your wife as Christ loved the church. Consider George Gilder's observation in *Men and Marriage*:

> It is men who make the major sacrifice. The man renounces his dream of short-term sexual freedom and self-fulfillment—his male sexuality and self-expression—in order to serve a woman

and family for a lifetime. It is a traumatic act of giving up his most profound yearning, his bent for the hunt and the chase, the motorbike and the open road, . . . and immediate excitements. . . . This male sacrifice . . . is essential to civilization.[2]

It sounds like a touch of what Christ did for humankind.

Looking Out for Her Interests

To love your wife as Christ loved the church, you're to regard her as more important than you are; you're to consider her sexual needs more important than yours.

The rest of the Ephesians 5 passage is a good reminder:

So husbands ought also to love their own wives as their own bodies. He who loves his own wife loves himself; for no one ever hated his own flesh, but nourishes and cherishes it, just as Christ also does the church, because we are members of His body. For this cause shall a man leave his father and mother, and shall cleave to his wife; and the two shall become one flesh. This mystery is great; but I am speaking with reference to Christ and the church.

Nevertheless let each individual among you also love his own wife even as himself; and let the wife see to it that she respect her husband (5:28-33).

So when you tell your wife you'd like to have sex and she'd rather sit and talk and cuddle, what do you do?

As the last chapter suggested, when you go her way, you bring out the best of her sexuality. So you talk and cuddle! But you can't go into the talking and cuddling with the selfish expectation that you'll get what you want. It won't work.

When you truly relinquish your wants, your deeper needs are met. Christ did not empty Himself and die on the cross so that He'd be exalted, but that's what happened:

> God also has highly exalted Him and given Him the name which is above every name, that at the name of Jesus every knee should bow, of those in heaven, and of those on earth, and of those under the earth (Philippians 2:9-10, NKJV).

When you get the focus off what you so desperately want, when you pay more attention to your wife's needs, sexual fulfillment will result.

Prepare Yourself for Her

Being a Christlike husband means being like Christ, the Bridegroom, is with the church, His bride. When the Bible talks about Christ coming for His bride (Revelation 21-22), it describes Him arriving in all His glory with armies in white robes. You probably won't approach your wife that way (though it could add humor to a tense situation). Still, preparing yourself for her can reflect loving her as Christ loves the church.

Here are three practical ways to get ready:

1. *Prepare your body.* During a sexual experience, you and your wife share your bodies most intimately. Coming to sex with a well-groomed body demonstrates your care and invites a positive response.

We recommend showering before sex, though not because we

believe the genitals are a dirty part of the body; they aren't. Having a clean body means getting rid of body odor and sweat and making sure you smell good and feel nice to be touched anywhere. Showering or bathing together can be a way to feel closer to each other as you begin to share your bodies.

Brushing your teeth and shaving before sex make kissing more pleasant. Bad breath is often reported by one spouse as the reason the couple has stopped kissing passionately—yet that spouse may never have told the other that halitosis was the problem. Since passionate kissing is a key to a vital sex life, spouses need to be honest with each other about their breath.

2. *Prepare your mind.* The brain is often referred to as the primary sexual organ, controlling response, attitudes, and feelings. Your mind-set will affect every sexual interaction, and each time will be different. What happened during the hours before, how you're feeling, what you think of the temperature and the look of the room will shape your time together.

Consider what you're bringing to the marital bed and how that might add to or distract from your time with your wife. Picture how you'd like to be with her. Think through where she may be coming from. Take time to talk about where each of you is mentally, and what each would like.

3. *Prepare your spirit.* Having sex is becoming one—not just physically and emotionally, but spiritually. Take time to clear barriers in your relationship with God and feel replenished. You'll be better able to give yourself to your wife and to accept and enjoy what she gives you.

You may find that beginning with a spiritual connection enhances the depth of your sexual bond. Try taking time to read a

Bible passage and pray together. Thank God for your sexual experience, and ask Him for all the joy and delight He intends for the two of you as you become one.

Give More

Christ gave Himself for the church. Giving shouldn't be done in order to get, but it's usually rewarding.

That's certainly true in the sexual realm. Not only can you learn to receive pleasure from the giving itself, but giving to your wife—serving her and caring about her—will warm her to give herself to you. Just as demand stifles, giving energizes.

> Marriage is a license to freedom without demand; marriage is not a license to possess and control.

Enjoy your rights and responsibilities in your sexual relationship. Learn to freely give her your body without demand for your response or hers. As you give without expectation, you'll get.

I am my beloved's,
And his desire is for me.
Come, my beloved, let us go out into the country,
Let us spend the night in the villages.
Let us rise early and go to the vineyards;
Let us see whether the vine has budded
And its blossoms have opened,
And whether the pomegranates have bloomed.
There I will give you my love
(Song of Solomon 7:10-12).

CHAPTER FIVE

SEX IS NOT A SPECTATOR SPORT

"It's no fun! Hers don't work! There is no response! All I can say is, what a shame! It's a waste!" exclaimed Mark.

He was frustrated with his wife's beautiful body because she didn't get aroused easily or regularly when he stimulated her genitals. He had difficulty enjoying intimacy with her; he watched for the response he could produce.

Watching for the result rather than focusing on the enjoyment of each other's bodies and the pleasure of being together will interfere with *attaining* the result.

Here's how it works.

If you're a Red Sox fan, you enjoy yourself when you watch your team play. Your body and emotions react to the ups and downs of the game. There's no pressure on you to perform.

> **When you're mentally outside looking in as you play in the game of sex, you will lose.**

But if you're playing church league baseball and watch yourself anxiously as you get up to bat, critiquing your own swing and stance, your enjoyment evaporates and your performance is likely to spiral downward.

Sex is something like that. Monitoring "how you're doing" usually interferes with your responses rather than heightening them.

YOU WATCHING YOU

You come home from work on a Friday evening. You've had a long week. You feel the tension between your wife and the kids when you walk in.

The baby-sitter will be there soon so you and your wife can go out to dinner, come home, and slip into the back bedroom without the kids knowing. But you're not looking forward to it. Sex hasn't been working too well for you lately; you get into it, then lose your responsiveness. You're starting to get concerned about your performance.

You're *spectatoring*. You've moved outside the experience, started watching your body's response, and hurt yourself and your time with your wife.

Response isn't nearly as important as the fun you and your wife can have and the love you feel when you're together. But it can be hard to convince yourself of that.

Once spectatoring has become a habit, it tends to control what you think and feel. It interrupts the natural flow. You start placing demands on yourself to get your body to work; the more pressure and concern you feel, the less likely your anatomy is to cooperate.

For sex to work, you need emotional abandon. It doesn't help to think about how your body is responding—whatever the reason.

Sometimes the reason is as simple as unrealistic expectations.

For example, a woman may complain to us about her husband's lack of ejaculatory control. We discover that she expects him to be able to thrust vigorously for 20 minutes without stopping or ejaculating—impossible for most men. Her unrealistic expectations have made him more and more anxious.

Another woman may think that her middle-aged husband should be able to have intercourse, ejaculate, and be restimulated to another erection without a rest period. Most men require 20 minutes to 20 hours for that process.

Or the man complains that he lacks sexual desire—because he expects to come to the sexual experience already erect. He mistakenly equates arousal with desire, not realizing that the latter usually precedes the former.

So your reproductive system may not be the problem. Fatigue, illness, stress, distraction, guilt, a critical wife, anxiety, depression, and medication all can interfere with your body's natural responses and start you watching yourself.

Eight Ways to Stop Spectatoring

Whatever the reason for its beginning, you can break spectatoring by removing all demands for your response and focusing on pleasure. To become an active player and stop watching yourself, try taking these steps:

1. *Don't insist on intercourse.* Sex doesn't equal intercourse. As Dr. Warwick Williams writes, "Lovemaking means literally that—interacting physically and emotionally. . . . Arousal, intercourse, and orgasm or ejaculation are nonessential, and simply possible lovemaking options."[1]

Stopping short of intercourse or orgasm for a while—not in a punitive, withholding way, but out of personal restraint—can teach you to savor the wonderful sensations of the moment instead of focusing on "results."

> The secret to stop spectatoring: Remove all demands for response and focus on the enjoyment of your bodies.

2. *Redefine good sex.* Don't let your definition of "success" depend on involuntary responses of your body that you can't control. Bernie Zilbergeld, Ph.D., said it well in *The New Male Sexuality*: "You're having good sex if you feel good about yourself, and good about your partner, and good about what you are doing. And later you have a good time of reflection."[2]

3. *Accept sexual anxiety as normal.* Practically every man will be anxious about sex sometime during his marriage. Young, newly married men will be anxious about their experience. Many men are anxious about penis size. Others are nervous about satisfying their wives. Middle-aged and older men may worry about erections and ejaculation.

When you accept anxiety as normal, it's less likely to overwhelm you. You realize that others have survived it, and you can, too.

4. *Define your conditions for sex.* If you need to be free of anxiety before engaging in sexual contact with your wife, tell her so. You may need to feel rested or safe and positively connected with your wife. It's reasonable to ask that the sexual time won't pose demands and unrealistic expectations.

5. *Distract yourself from evaluating bodily responses.* Get lost in each other. Talk to your wife about your enjoyment of her body; it's a great affirmation as well as a distraction.

6. *Focus on pleasing sensations.* Soak in the touch as you're

caressing and being caressed. Enjoy her body for your pleasure; allow her to enjoy yours in the same way. Experiment with a variety of touches; choose objects with different textures, like silk or feathers, to caress. Use your penis like a paintbrush to bring pleasure to her genitals without entry.

7. *Talk about your fears.* One way to defuse negative thoughts is to speak them as soon as you're aware of them. For example, let's say you and your wife are getting ready for sexual contact. You think, *What if I lose it tonight?* Tell her immediately. Verbalizing helps to break the control a thought can have over your body.

8. *Picture positive sexual feelings, actions, and responses.* When negative images enter your mind, try to let them go. The more you rehearse the positive and eliminate the negative, the more quickly your experiences will be filled with warm, loving passion.

WATCHING HER

Ever watch a hovering boss or a smothering mom? Every move the employee or child makes is met with an evaluation or question:

"Oh, are you going to put it in *that* account?"

"Don't you think it would work better if you started with this problem?"

"I notice you didn't get finished with your project yesterday."

"You'd do better if you did it this way."

Some men are hovering lovers. The more the husband hovers, the less the wife can experience her sexuality. She gets discouraged, feels diminishing interest in sex, and has fewer and less intense sexual responses. In return, seeing her as a problem to fix, he makes more and more "loving" suggestions. He's watching her, and now she's watching herself.

Carol and Allen had completed the sexual therapy process to treat what they had defined as her lack of sexual desire and decreased sexual arousal and release. Discovering that he was watching her, we'd helped him look at why her sexuality was so important to his emotional security. They'd retrained themselves to get the focus off her sexuality and onto the pleasure of being together, and now they were having good sexual times.

Then Carol called for help. They were both discouraged. She hadn't been "in the mood" for several weeks. A sexy outfit hadn't helped. Neither had "hoping the feelings would follow the actions" as we "had taught them." Once she did get in the mood briefly, but slipped out of it when Allen had to get up and close the shades. The next time they had intercourse, he stopped thrusting and suggested that if she would move, that would probably help her "get into it." He then said, "You're not trying." She got furious.

Carol told us she was feeling stubborn. She didn't want to do the things she knew would help. Her old resistance had been rekindled by Allen's evaluations of her body's responses.

Fortunately, the two of them remembered the principles they'd learned. Their slide back into old habits brought laughter and the ability to reaffirm and reapply those ideas.

If you're hovering, you need to stop. Don't watch your wife and judge her sexuality! If your ability to enjoy yourself during sex depends on her involuntary responses, her body will never respond. Your monitoring will interfere.

Ways to Stop Watching Her

Just knowing about the problem won't solve it, of course. Here are some tangible efforts you can make:

1. *Deliberately affirm her.* Tell her what you enjoy about her body—how it looks, how good it feels when it touches you and you touch it. Don't concentrate on how it responds or moves or *does* anything; just focus on what it *is.*

2. *Distract yourself.* If watching is a habit for you, direct your gaze elsewhere for a while. Look into her eyes; study her hair; count the squares on the quilt if you have to.

3. *Focus on the sensations of touch.* Explore every skin surface, every crevice. Don't analyze them; just enjoy how wonderful they feel.

KEEPING SCORE

It was February of 1977. A couple asked us for help. They'd been married 20 years and had a wonderful sex life until October 1976, when the husband started having trouble maintaining erections.

That was America's bicentennial year, 1976. The couple had decided to celebrate by having sex 200 times that year. This is a true story! October arrived, and they realized they'd had sex only 85 times; they had 115 to go, and only 3 months to reach their goal. Keeping score became a pressure; it was no longer a fun project.

No wonder he was having problems.

> **Whenever sex becomes goal oriented, the body's responses will be affected, and enjoyment will be stifled.**

Whenever sex becomes goal oriented, the body's responses will be affected, and enjoyment will be stifled.

Counting sexual experiences or responses doesn't just happen during bicentennial celebrations. It can be the result of an anxious partner, a demanding spouse, infertility struggles, clearing sperm from the system after a vasectomy, or setting a goal for any reason. Once you start keeping score, the focus is off the process and on the quota. The efforts to reach that quota are often destructive.

Some years ago, a month before our last child was born, Cliff had a vasectomy. The short time between his surgery and the delivery of Kristine left little opportunity or energy for Cliff to have enough ejaculations to ensure that the sperm were out of his system by the time we were ready to resume our sexual life. So we started counting ejaculations. You can guess what happened!

You may have started counting for reasons of your own. You may be tallying how often you've had sex, how long you've lasted, how many orgasms your wife had, and who initiated what.

Whatever you're counting, you can be sure that response will fade away. You can take charge of your sexual experience and make some things happen, but you can't stand back and keep score.

QUESTIONING

Questioning is a form of hovering, watching, and comparing:
"Was that good for you, honey?"
"Are you feeling anything?"
"Are you in the mood?"
"What about tonight?"
"Would you like to?"
Each question represents an expectation without taking personal responsibility to express what you want.

A man usually asks these questions because he wants to know how well he's doing. They reflect the idea that sex is a competition. Indirectly, the man is asking, "How many points did I get on this one? Did I measure up?" The competition may be against a real or imaginary lover, a standard, or the woman herself.

Interrogation intrudes. It provokes defensiveness instead of promoting acceptance, enjoyment, and sharing of yourself.

Ask Me No Questions

When it comes to initiating sex, let her know what you'd like and respect her response. Don't ask whether she'd like to make love, thereby putting the pressure on her.

Instead of asking, "Would you give me a kiss?" just kiss her. Start gently.

Instead of asking, "What about tonight?" lure her with, "I'd like to play tonight."

Instead of "Are you in the mood?" say something like, "Boy, am I in the mood!"

During the sexual experience, avoid asking how it's going for her.

Rather than asking, "Does this feel good?" reveal your own feelings: "Wow, does this feel good!"

Rather than "Are you feeling anything?" try, "I could do this forever."

Rather than "Am I in the right spot?" say, "For me, that's the most wonderful spot."

Afterward, try not to evaluate the experience. Affirm it.

Replace "Was that good for you?" with "I sure enjoyed you."

Replace "Did you have an orgasm?" with "That was an explosive one for me. Hope I didn't leave you behind."

Replace "Did I do better that time?" with "I felt more comfortable that time."

Questions can be a way of protecting yourself. They keep you out of the spotlight and shine it on her. They're a form of spectatoring.

The sooner you can catch and change spectatoring habits, the freer you'll find sex to be.

Take the risk; be a player. Sure, you could get hurt. But you also could stir up a lot of ecstasy.

And wouldn't that be worth the risk?

CHAPTER SIX

SEX: A PATH TO INTIMACY

Sexual needs are changing. We find fewer couples seeking help for "technical difficulties" like impotence, premature ejaculation, and orgasmic inhibition. More people are using self-help books to deal with these issues in the privacy of the bedroom.

But one thing hasn't changed: Couples are still desperately seeking help to overcome the intimacy barriers in their sexual relationships. And when they do, they see differences accepted, find demands relieved, and discover new levels of love and passion.

Intimacy isn't just a "women's problem." In this chapter, we'll look at how roadblocks to closeness can affect you, too.

WHEN HER SEXUALITY = YOUR MALENESS

If you believe your masculinity depends on your wife's responses, you're headed for trouble. Since a woman's sexuality is unpredictable, relying on her desire for you isn't a great way to build the security that lets intimacy grow.

When your self-worth rests on your ability to sexually fulfill your wife, you'll both feel pressured to achieve that goal. A woman's sexual enjoyment is naturally fulfilling to a man, but a focus on getting her response in order to validate you will decrease pleasure for both spouses. It can destroy passion as well as intimacy.

> Sex won't be great when your self-worth depends on your wife's sexual responsiveness; love, passion, and intimacy will be destroyed.

Go for Less, Not More

Your wife's sexual enthusiasm can be derailed by your eagerness, especially when it's born of insecurity or the need to prove yourself. That's the reason for our "lag behind" rule. If you keep your sexual intensity and activity just less than your wife's, she'll be hungry for more.

Sexual anorexia in a woman is often a response to having been "force-fed" by an overeager husband. It's a little like setting out food for young children. If you don't give them much, they cry for more. If you overload their plates, they play with their food and seem disinterested in eating.

Keep your wife hungry, but not starving. Enjoy every inch of her body before you go near the hot spots.

Stroke her slowly everywhere for your enjoyment, not for the response your touching produces. Let her invite more direct stimulation. Don't resist when she invites; respond to her invitation with delight.

What if she never feels secure enough to invite? Work out a signal so that you can know when she's ready for more. Err on the side of waiting too long rather than pursuing too soon.

If your instincts carry you away and you revert to pursuing too fast and too intensely, back off as soon as you notice her tighten up. We have a game that we enjoy when Cliff's aggression is too intense for Joyce. Cliff starts playing hard to get:

"Oh, no, I'm really too tired tonight."

"That's way too intense for me; can we slow down?"

"Do we have to?"

It's an instant cure. It adds fun and triggers Joyce's ardor.

DESTRUCTIVE RELATIONSHIP PATTERNS

Most spouses we see in sexual therapy long to be loved intimately. But they struggle with relationship discord, shame and control issues, anger, abuse, and fears of abandonment that block closeness and damage their sexual lives.

It doesn't have to be this way. Let's look at some of the most common intimacy blockers and how to get rid of them.

When Your Need for Validation Is Spelled S-E-X

For many men, sex releases tension, helps them feel good about themselves, and opens them to experience love with their wives. But the man who needs sex just to feel good about himself has crossed a line into a "neediness" that stifles enjoyment for both.

If you need sex for validation, you probably entered marriage lacking confidence when it comes to women. Maybe you didn't date much before meeting your wife. You might be sensitive to rejection because of your history with women, or because you didn't get unconditional love from your mother, or because you and your father lacked a strong connection.

You probably feel your wife doesn't desire you as much as she used to. But because of your sensitivity to rejection, she can never want you enough to fill that void inside you.

For your wife, sex has changed from something she wanted to something you need from her. She's ended up performing out of duty, or resisting your neediness, or withdrawing completely.

This destructive relationship pattern causes sex to be more than sex. It may continue until you get professional help, separate, or resign yourself to a hobbled sex life.

Fortunately, there's a solution. It's twofold: (1) Separate your need for validation from your wife's sexuality, and (2) affirm any evidence of her sexuality. Her sexuality will resurface and validate you.

You'll probably need the support of a therapist to make the process work. Your goal will be to eliminate your need to be validated by sex. Then you'll be able to fulfill the command of 1 Corinthians 7 to mutually and freely enjoy each other.

When Your Performance Is Necessary to Validate Her

Women sometimes have a similar need to be validated through sex. For example, your wife may feel you don't care about her if you can't delay your ejaculation for an unrealistically long time, get an erection without stimulation, be restimulated after ejaculation, or enable her to have an orgasm during intercourse. To feel loved, she must have your sexual response on her terms.

If this is the case, your wife probably was hurt by men during her childhood. She's looking for proof that you won't hurt her. Finding it hard to trust you, she sets standards that are almost impossible to meet.

The skills of a professional counselor would help her and take the pressure off you. Your strength can also help.

Separate what you can do for her from what you can't. Reassure her with words and actions that you love her, you'll be there for her, and you won't violate her. But make it clear that you can't do the physically impossible—regaining an erection immediately after ejaculation, for instance. Let her know that your physical inability to meet her performance demands has nothing to do with your care for her.

> **Separate what you can do for your wife from what you can't; affirm your love without conforming to her performance demands.**

When Anger Interrupts Intimacy

Intimacy can be frightening. So frightening, in fact, that anger seems safer.

That may be hard to believe. But if anger is blocking closeness to your wife, consider the possibility that you're choosing anger over intimacy.

Anger can spring from a personal problem. One man constantly belittled and distrusted his wife's sexuality because his mother had hurt his father by having an affair. As a young boy, he'd become his father's confidant and helper in catching his mother in action.

Another man was angry with his mother over the way she frequently pushed his father away. This man's wife was sexually suppressed, but he couldn't see his part in it and left therapy.

Other men are angry because of physical abuse or emotional

neglect by their fathers. Whatever the source, the anger is brought into the sexual relationship and used passively or actively to destroy intimacy.

Anger can be triggered in the relationship, too. Paul and Patricia had been married only six months when they called for our help. Neither of them had a positive word to say about the other. Trying to focus on their sexual relationship was like treating a cut on the hand when the person is going into heart failure.

When we gave them sexual retraining assignments, they didn't complete any of them. Anger interrupted the process.

For some couples, anger shows up only in sex. She resists sex because he pushes her to have it; he complains because she resists. His expression of sexual need makes her angry; her lack of need makes him angry.

When both partners understand how anger is wrecking their relationship and make their differences work for them, they can reverse their destructive pattern. Then anger dissipates and intimacy builds.

We worked with a couple who found this to be true. After 30 years of his pushing and her resisting, they were ready to dissolve their marriage. We were their last-ditch effort.

In time we discovered something that neither had ever told the other: Both had been sexually abused as children. With their permission, we shared that information in a feedback session. The revelation brought a caring response from each to the other. The walls were down; it was the beginning of their building a mutually satisfying sexual relationship.

With similar counseling, you and your wife can overcome anger and do the same.

When Control Issues Keep Sex Safe

Just as some people use anger to avoid intimacy, others use control.

In fact, control may seem even safer than anger in protecting you from intimacy with your wife. When she wants you sexually, you find it difficult to respond—always, of course, with a valid reason. Still, you complain because the two of you aren't having sex as often as you'd like.

> Control may seem even safer than anger in protecting you from your fear of intimacy.

Control may block sexual intimacy in other ways, too. For example, let's say your wife doesn't want sex with you because you ejaculate prematurely. But she refuses to do exercises with you in order to help you learn ejaculatory control. That protects her from the vulnerability of intimacy.

In our practice, control issues often surface in the form of resisting sexual retraining. The couple or individual comes to resolve a sexual problem, but won't work the program. The stated reasons are lack of discipline, not enough time, doubting it will work, already knowing what we're trying to tell them, and similar excuses.

You may also be controlling because you're afraid to be totally yourself in your wife's presence. Maybe being yourself wasn't safe when you were a child, and now it's virtually impossible to be open and vulnerable during sex. If your wife is critical or lacks unconditional love, the problem is even more pronounced.

You long for closeness, but can't risk letting it happen. If you seek help, you find reasons not to complete the process.

There is hope, if you commit yourself to working through the problem with a counselor. The steps toward intimacy need to be small and in your control, so that you can risk taking them.

PERSONAL ISSUES

Shame

When sex is associated with shame, it interferes with sexual passion in marriage.

As one woman said, "I was so sexual before marriage that we had intense struggles keeping from having intercourse. I shut down when I was standing at the altar saying my vows. The thought hit me: *I can't imagine others knowing that now that we are married we will be having sex.*"

Years later, that woman and her husband still had not had sex. She had involuntarily closed up the muscle that controls the opening of the vagina, and he was not able to penetrate her. In her case, shame had begun when, as a young girl, she'd responded sexually to her father's pornography.

Shame associated with sex may start with other kinds of premature or inappropriate sexual exposure, too. A young boy may have shared a bed with his mother or older sister; a child may have slept in the same room while the parents carried on their sexual relationship; an adolescent daughter may have been seen by her father when she was nude; or the child's innocence and sexual development were otherwise not protected.

Shame is a heavy burden to carry. Breaking the connection between it and sex usually takes deliberate work with a therapist, followed by positive step-by-step building of sex in marriage. That effort will bring greater joy and freedom to your sex life.

Abandonment

Having been abandoned makes it difficult to be intimate. If you were abandoned during the first year of your life, for example, the capacity for sexual intimacy may have to be learned in marriage.

Abandonment can be physical or emotional. Perhaps you were adopted and didn't bond with your adoptive mother and father until after age one. Or your mother or primary caregiver was hospitalized for a long time during that first year. Or other factors—depression, grief, an inability to be close and warm—caused your mother to be emotionally absent.

Maybe you lost a parent before you were thirteen or fourteen. The death of a parent, especially the opposite-sex parent, can cause extreme difficulty in allowing sexual intimacy with one's spouse. One man whose mother died of diabetes during his preschool years would fall asleep or lose his erection when he got involved sexually with his wife.

The path to intimacy from abandonment is a tough climb up a steep mountain. Intimacy is the opposite of abandonment; the fear of intimacy is the fear of abandonment. With professional help, trust must be built with a secure, giving spouse who is uncommonly consistent and emotionally available.

> **Since abuse is a violation of trust, it interrupts the natural ability for intimacy in marriage.**

Abuse

Whether the abuse was physical, emotional, or sexual, you learned that being close isn't safe. Without safety, being sexually intimate in marriage is exceedingly difficult.

If you've been abused, you still may be able to have intercourse.

But pleasuring and sharing your inner world will take willingness to risk and careful training.

Victims of sexual abuse describe a distinct pattern. As children, they either withdrew and felt shame or were aggressive and angry. They felt different from other kids. They report having had heightened sexual awareness as children; they tend to be promiscuous or at least highly interested outside marriage, and to shut down sexually as they approach marriage or soon after.

Overcoming abuse and bonding intimately in marriage is a rewarding process. Finally you can get the love you desperately want. But you need to work through the pain of the abuse.

You can do that by talking with a therapist or a support group of other abuse victims. The scars may not go away, but deep and intimate sexual fulfillment is definitely attainable.

Poor Self-Esteem

Do you feel uncomfortable with your body? You may be attractive by others' standards, but see only flaws in yourself. Those feelings may make it hard for you to take responsibility for sex and may keep you from sexually affirming your wife.

> Not feeling good about yourself or your body may make it difficult for you to take responsibility for sex and to sexually validate your wife.

Body image is just one factor shaping self-esteem. A negative self-image can come from many sources. Whatever the reason, the person who suffers in this way hasn't experienced the personal validation he needs to believe in himself.

Self-esteem can grow in a loving, committed marriage. A wife who touches you in nondemanding ways can help you feel accepted and help you accept yourself and your body. You can take action to improve aspects of your body, personality, and skills that increase your personal positive regard. More importantly, you can consider the fact that as God's creation, you're of tremendous value to Him.

If you need help with self-worth issues, don't hesitate to consult a counselor or pastor. As you gain confidence, you can take more responsibility for your sexual relationship and to respect the sexuality of your wife. Sex will become an expression of your good feelings about yourself and your wife, and will be marked by true intimacy.

Addiction

Sexual addictions counteract sexual intimacy.

In an addiction, the stimulus for arousal and release is outside the person and usually outside an intimate relationship. Rather than losing himself with his wife, the man sells himself to pornographic magazines or Internet sites, cross-dressing, prostitution, affairs, or other actions that falsely promise to fulfill the deep cry within him that seeks satisfaction through sexual intensity and release.

The man who's sexually addicted may find that even though it's lonely to masturbate while watching a video, he can be himself with the inanimate resource. There's no risk of intimacy and losing himself.

We'll have more to say about sexual addictions in Chapter 13. If you struggle with an addiction, enlist the aid of a professional counselor. You'll find that the avenue to filling the hunger inside you—to be completely and freely loved by another human for who you are—is a truly intimate relationship with your wife.

> Therefore a man shall leave his father and mother and be joined to his wife, and they shall become one flesh (Genesis 2:24, NKJV).

CHAPTER SEVEN

WHEN SEX ISN'T WORKING

All couples' sex lives are disrupted from time to time. We've struggled with several bouts of difficulty ourselves.

The first was after our honeymoon. Joyce's enthusiastic pursuit of Cliff probably triggered performance pressure. That was quickly alleviated when Joyce backed off.

The next dilemma was pain for Joyce after our first child was born. It continued, causing decreased interest, until after our second child was born 22 months later.

As we've already mentioned, counting ejaculations after a vasectomy brought back the performance pressure of our early marriage.

> **Temporary disruption of sexual functioning is normal.**

And then there have been all those times when plain old life circumstances caused dry spells.

Maybe you've had similar struggles, all of which are normal. Maybe you were able to work them out without professional help.

On the other hand, perhaps you needed assistance. Perhaps you need it now.

Some of the problems in this chapter might be addressed by

following the advice of a self-help book; others nearly always require the help of a therapist. In any case, when a pattern of disruption in your sexual life persists longer than a month or two, it's probably time to seek outside help.

Asking for help is seen by many men as a sign of weakness. But avoiding the pain will be well worth it.

When a sexual struggle invades your relationship, it attacks your self-esteem—and your wife's. As you feel worse about yourselves, both of you will respond with characteristic weaknesses. You may withdraw, become more aggressive, deliver put-downs, show frustration or anger, or otherwise damage your relationship.

> **Sexual failure perpetuates more failure; intervention interrupts failure.**

Sexual dilemmas have a way of perpetuating themselves. Long after the initial cause of the difficulty has passed, the predicament may persist.

Failure elicits more failure. Spouses avoid each other because they don't want to fail again. When they finally do connect, both are anxious and feel pressure to succeed. The likelihood of success lessens, and the problem grows.

Don't put off getting help when you need it. The cost of asking will be more than repaid by the benefits.

TWENTY-ONE WAYS NOT TO LOVE YOUR LOVER

Is it possible that you're part of the problem? See whether you recognize yourself on this list, and consider our suggestions for improving the situation.

#1: *The Naive Lover*

We described this guy in Chapter 2. If you were shy, withdrawn, or restricted from interacting with girls, this may be you.

When you finally married your wife, you may have felt awkward in your physical interaction with her. Being sexual didn't flow easily for you. The unfamiliar art of passionate kissing left you uncomfortable and her wanting. You may have felt overly modest around her.

Your wife may sometimes give you the message, even though she's probably kind about it, that you don't quite know what you're doing. You don't know how to be with a woman in a way that satisfies her sexually.

If this is you, take heart. The fastest learners we work with in sexual therapy are the naive men. You're like an empty sponge, ready to soak up information.

In addition to this book, many self-help resources are available (see the back of this book for a list of our own). You and your wife can work through a book like *Restoring the Pleasure* or watching a video series like *The Magic and Mystery of Sex*. Attending a seminar on sexuality will saturate you with input and speed up your learning curve. You and your wife will be delighted with the rewards of learning fast and retaining what you've learned.

#2: *The Goal-Oriented Lover*

The first type of lover in this category is the entrepreneur. By that we mean that he sets goals, works toward them, accomplishes them, and moves on to new ones.

Marriage may have been one of those goals. He set out to find a wonderful wife, court her in style, and get his family and home established. Now, though, he's moved on to the next project.

This approach may work well when you're starting a company or building a church. But your wife won't be happy to be the project left behind.

If you want a marriage that includes a sexually fulfilling relationship, you need to change your goal. Allow your entrepreneurial style to work for you by making your relationship with your wife a priority.

Decide that you're going to be your wife's lover. Design into your schedule the amount of connecting and sharing time that will serve her and maintain a joyful sexual life. Try our recommendation of fifteen minutes per day, one evening per week, one day per month, and one weekend per season.

The second type in the "goal-oriented" category is the watchful lover. We described him in Chapter 5. He watches to see whether his wife is getting aroused, if she's lubricating, if her nipples are erect, if he has an erection, if sex is taking too long, if she's reaching the same level of ecstasy that she has in the past, if she's having an orgasm. These goals get in the way of the natural, loving process of two people becoming one.

If you're a watchful lover, shift from achieving goals to getting lost in the pleasure. Or to put it another way, make mutual pleasure your goal.

#3: The Bored Lover

Has sex become routine? Are you bored with the repetition? Is the way you make love the same as it was five years ago or fifteen years ago?

Maybe you see yourself as a singularly uncreative person.

You want to change, but wouldn't know how to experiment even if you felt free to do so. Trying anything different would make you feel vulnerable or anxious.

For you, change will have to be deliberate. Start by talking about your concern with your wife. Then come up with a plan, however simple it may be. Sometimes even shifting the way you lie in bed, so that your head is at the foot, can bring a whole new perspective.

A change in location can provide a new spark, too. You might make love on the floor or in the guest bedroom. Switching roles as the "active" one will make a major difference. See Chapter 11 for more ideas.

If trying anything new is a paralyzing idea, it may help to do some self-exploration. Writing, journaling, or individual psychotherapy can help you open yourself up to the one person to whom you've committed to share yourself at this deep level.

#4: The Insecure Lover

Insecure lovers struggle with low self-esteem. They respond in one direction or the other: Either they're passive and compliant, never expressing their needs or expectations, or they're directly or indirectly demanding and insistent. Neither leaves the woman feeling the quiet confidence she's looking for in the man she loves.

Changing how you feel about yourself can be a lifelong project. But you and your wife will find some immediate relief when you identify that your sexual stresses are due to your insecurity.

Once you do that, you can consciously work on aspects of yourself that you can control. You can improve your appearance, vocabulary, or habits, for example.

Letting yourself be vulnerable enough to share and work on this issue with your wife will draw the two of you together. That can be the most important step toward becoming a more secure lover.

#5: The Sloppy Lover

This guy hasn't learned to care. Maybe he grew up in a home that didn't attend to the details of civilized living, or he may have rejected his mother's nagging.

If you're a sloppy lover, you may be ignoring your bodily preparation for the sexual experience. The unwashed, unshaven man with poor oral hygiene rarely appeals to a woman. If you've rationalized that her complaints about you are her problem, you need to understand that *every woman needs a clean man!*

Sometimes sloppiness is a matter of carelessness in lovemaking. Are you paying attention to where your elbow is landing, to what you say, to how you move your or her body? You'll probably know if you're a sloppy lover by listening to the gentle—or not so gentle—comments your wife makes.

Our advice: Do something about your sloppiness, and do it now! You won't talk your wife into accepting your sloppiness as part of your wonderfully quirky personality.

The wife of a sloppy lover feels uncared for and disregarded. Taking action will help your wife know that you value her.

#6: The Codependent Lover

The "codependent" label has become popular and overused, but it's helpful here. The codependent person feeds off another person's pathology.

The codependent husband keeps his wife's resistance to sex

going by grumbling and complaining about her lack of desire. She "needs" him to be grumbling or negative toward her so that she doesn't want to have sex with him; he "needs" her to be sexually resistant so he can grumble and complain. It's almost a dance.

Has a pattern like this been established between the two of you? Do you play your part and know it well? Would you find it hard to function without the ongoing provocation or complaint or sadness that seems to be between you?

If you're unhappy with your sexual relationship and blame each other, you may be perpetuating such a pattern. The sexual difficulty serves some purpose for you, even though you're adamant that you don't like things the way they are.

Since the pattern feeds itself, it's difficult to break. You may need the help of a strong therapist. His or her challenge will be to get both spouses' sides of the pattern under control at the same time, long enough for each to see hope for change.

You could help bring change by stopping your negativity and starting to affirm your wife. Focus on any positive, no matter how small. Almost inevitably, her sexual resistance will decrease. By stopping your complaints, you give her no excuse to resist.

#7: The Avoidant Lover

The avoidant lover may be unsure of himself. He may be naive. He may have been hurt in a past situation. Or he may be self-conscious about his body or his penis size.

Concern about penis size begins in preadolescence and can continue into adulthood. Penis size has little or nothing to do with a man's ability to satisfy a woman, since the vagina can accommodate any size penis—and the pleasurable sensations are only in the lower one and one-half to two inches of the vagina. Besides, most erect penises are close to equal. Still, apprehension about penis size is one reason a man avoids his wife.

Another reason is fear of being vulnerable with a woman. It may seem too much of an emotional risk to reach out and engage in a sexual experience. The husband may prefer to reach for the TV remote!

If you and your wife clash over who should get the sexual experience started, or if your wife is angry with you for not meeting her sexual needs, you may be an avoidant lover.

How does this affect your wife? She may demand sex, which will only exaggerate your need to pull away. In some ways that's what you want, because closeness is uncomfortable.

An avoidant lover might use masturbation as his sexual outlet. It's less hassle than a relationship, you don't have to fear rejection, you're less likely to fail, and you don't have to risk intimacy.

Avoidance will not change without deliberate effort. Your wife needs to stop pursuing; you need to initiate sexual contact on a designated, regular basis. You can't wait until you feel like initiating sex with your wife. All masturbation must stop, so that your bodily urges will nudge you to take action with your wife.

If sex with your wife has seemed like too much work, talk with her about your conditions for sexual pleasure. Build self-assurance and comfort with intimacy and initiation through a planned system of sexual contact.

#8: The Lazy Lover
Making an effort and delaying immediate gratification for long-term benefit work best in life. Not all men have developed this pattern in their sexual lives, though.

If you don't find the effort of connecting with your wife or delaying your ejaculation worth the long-term benefits of a mutually satisfying sexual relationship, you're probably a lazy lover.

Is it too much of a hassle to talk with her, touch her, and get her feeling good about you? Is it too hard to stroke her body in general, then stimulate her clitoris for 20 minutes? Are you unwilling to go through what it takes? Would you like it best if you could give her a cursory rub, followed by the proverbial "Wham, bam, thank you, ma'am"?

If so, there probably is little mutual pleasure in your sexual times; your laziness precludes any possibility of bonding or deep connection. You don't have a satisfying sexual life because you're not willing to take the time to meet her physical and emotional needs.

Your lack of motivation will be the biggest barrier to changing your lazy lover pattern. You have to decide to go against what is natural for you and take a few small steps toward delaying immediate gratification for deeper satisfaction.

With your wife, try writing a step-by-step plan listing the requirements for all sexual encounters. For example, the two of you might specify that you spend twenty minutes talking before you do any touching, then ten minutes of kissing and caressing before you take off any clothes. You might even use an electronic timer.

Normally, we're against such a programmed approach to sex. But for the lazy lover, a specific design planned with your wife will bring amazing benefits.

#9: The Angry Lover
You may have brought anger from your past into your marriage— anger toward parents, siblings, schoolmates, the army, a boss,

God, or whomever. Or the anger may stem from your marriage relationship.

Perhaps you've never dealt with marital hurts in a way that lets you move away from them and feel free of their impact. The anger finds its way into your marriage bed. You may express it directly with critical comments or actions, or passively by creating sexual distance.

An anger problem is best worked out with a therapist, not taken to bed. We also highly recommend Dr. Neil Clark Warren's book *Make Anger Your Ally* (Tyndale House Publishers, 1990). You can work through the process of identifying the type and source of your anger, then learn how to use that energy for your benefit rather than expressing it in ways that damage you and your relationship.

If your anger leads to verbal or physical abuse or causes you to be hurtful in the sexual experience, get help immediately. Anger that's out of control and being used to hurt is a serious crisis. Intervention is necessary to change the destructive pattern forever. It's never right, helpful, justified, or permissible for anger to come out in ways that demean or harm.

#10: The Possessive Lover

The possessive lover is the jealous lover.

Jealousy eats away at you like wood termites on a sycamore tree. It stifles love and interrupts the natural flow of sexual abandonment.

Your wife isn't yours to possess; she's a gift of God to freely enjoy, delight in, and give yourself to. Sexually, she needs to be free to give herself to you—to carry out the biblical instruction that each spouse's body is the other's. She can't freely say "Yes" without being totally free to say "No."

Husbands let jealousy interfere with their sex lives for a number of reasons. Most common is preoccupation with a former lover—one the wife had before marriage, often before husband and wife ever met. We hear this every day in our offices, and it affirms to us God's standard of saving sex for marriage. The couple may have been married for ten years, but the husband is still haunted by the thought of his wife having been with someone else. During sex, any pause or apparent lack of enthusiasm can trigger his jealous concern. He may be obsessed with getting the details of her history, unable to leave her past buried where it needs to be.

Or the husband's jealousies may be more current. Perhaps he's preoccupied with his wife's boss, choir director, or tennis instructor. The obsession isn't based on inappropriate behavior between the other man and his wife; it stems from the husband's anxiety.

He may even be jealous of their children, her mother, or her best friend, focusing on how much of her time and attention they get. Unless he feels he is the center of her life, he becomes nervous.

> She can't freely say "Yes" to sex until she can freely say "No."

Tom and Brenda had been married for 14 years. Tom couldn't seem to stop thinking about how Brenda had been sexually involved with a man before she'd made a commitment to Christ and before meeting Tom. Regularly Tom would review with her the activities of that past involvement. He asked for details, saying he didn't want any future surprises. Brenda tried to appease him with as much information as she could remember.

After every sexual encounter Tom and Brenda had, he doubted it had been as good as hers with the previous man. Tom's obsession was destroying the joy he could have been experiencing with his wife.

We had to help Tom accept that Brenda had been cleansed spiritually and mentally from her past. His jealousy was the only current difficulty with that past.

> **The security of commitment brings sexual freedom; possessiveness stifles it.**

When a husband's possessiveness isn't about what his wife is actually doing, it's about the lack of trust and the insecurity he brought into the relationship. If you're a possessive husband, you must get control of that jealousy. Otherwise, you'll drive your wife away rather than drawing her to you.

Seek help to understand the source of your jealousy. The security of commitment brings sexual freedom in marriage; possessiveness stifles it.

#11: The Selfish Lover

This guy is self-centered in bed—and usually in the rest of life, too.

If you focus on your needs and have difficulty caring about those of your wife, you're probably a selfish lover. Listen to your words. Do you say, "I need," "I want," "You should," and "If only you would"?

Maybe you think you just know what you want, or that you have refined taste. Or that if you can get her to meet your needs, then you'll be free to meet hers.

The selfish lover has a "me first" attitude. But the "me first" approach to sex doesn't work; sex will be the best for both of you when you're the servant leader, the servant lover, and the servant husband.

Repentance and a change of attitude are necessary to reverse selfishness. This habit dies slowly unless it's submitted to Christ and He's on the throne of your life.

Your wife can be a big help, too. Set aside a time to hear from her, without being defensive, what it's like to be connected with you as a selfish lover. If you can face yourself, you may then have the knowledge, courage, and strength, with God's help, to change.

#12: The Passive Lover

While the selfish lover is *actively* self-centered, the passive lover is *inactively* self-centered. He says, "Let her do it."

This husband has little capacity to give; he wants to be pleased. He's a one-way sponge that only takes in. One wife described her passive-lover husband this way: He would prepare for lovemaking by lying on the bed, putting his hands behind his head, and signaling that he was ready for her to begin.

> You are special, but so is your wife; relinquish your rights to be served and serve her.

The passive lover believes he's special, so he needs to be attended to in a special way. There's a touch of royalty in this kind of passive self-centeredness. He may feel that his wife is lucky to have him— someone so charming, bright, attractive, rich, musical, whatever. She should be grateful, he thinks; if she isn't, lots of other women would be.

This attitude has a way of making others, especially the wife, feel inadequate and eventually very angry. The wife may try at first to please the passive lover, but she reaches the point of despair or fury. She feels violated.

Like the selfish lover, the passive lover requires a change of heart. If you fall into this category, you can't continue to assume that you're special and exempt from the normal expectations of the husband-wife relationship. Your approach has been the antithesis of servant leadership. It's not easy to change, but it's essential if you're going to have a fulfilling sexual life.

#13: The Critical Lover

The critical lover evaluates, with a hostile edge. His reviews may not be limited to sex. He may knock his wife's housekeeping, appearance, weight, clothes, decorating, childrearing, or the way she irons trousers.

During sex, he criticizes the way she moves or doesn't move, whether or not she shows the right degree of enthusiasm, or whether she responds at the right speed. This process stifles spontaneity and joy.

If you're a critical lover, put-downs may seem to come automatically to you. Perhaps one of your parents was this way with you when you were growing up.

Correcting your critical nature may start by controlling your tongue before you get control of your mind. Decide not to say what you think; better not to say anything than to put your wife down. Practice replacing the critical thought with a positive one.

As your wife hears positives from you, you'll be rewarded by her enjoyment. That, in turn, will elicit more positives from you. Eventually you'll find that even your thinking will be less judgmental.

#14: The Controlling Lover

This man feels the need to control his wife. When it comes to sex, he may want to be in charge of the sequence, the activities, even the response. Sex has to be on his terms. If it isn't, he gets anxious and sabotages it.

The controlling lover may want power over only certain aspects of the sexual experience, or may "clamp down" only when he feels his wife or the event is "out of control." If he feels anxious or insecure about his response or performance, he may try to manage his shakiness by trying to take charge.

If you're a controlling lover, you're probably getting one of two responses. Your wife is passively going along and losing interest— or she's fighting you for control every step of the way.

Letting go may be tough for you. Start by identifying what triggers your need for control. Talk about it with your wife. Encourage her to let you know when your controlling tendencies are interfering with your sex life.

Try an experiment: Let her take charge of an entire sexual experience. It might even be fun. Tell her your thoughts as you're in the passive role.

As you learn to focus on mutual pleasure, you'll discover the relief that comes with being able to release your firm grip.

#15: The Distant Lover

This man avoids intimacy; he remains aloof. He has to keep his distance, not only from his wife, but also from himself.

> Know yourself, open your heart, share yourself, and the comfort of closeness with your wife will follow.

The distant lover struggles with a lack of self-acceptance, which he's learned to manage by projecting aloofness. Others may think he's self-confident or even stuck up, but his standoffishness is about his discomfort with intimacy.

There's usually a good reason why a lover is distant. If you're in this category, you may have experienced either pain or coldness from your parents while growing up. You may have been hurt when you allowed yourself to be open in a previous relationship. You may have encountered hurtful peers as a child.

Whatever the reason, your distance interferes with your sex life. For example, you might regularly ask questions of your wife during lovemaking. With you in the inquiring role and her as respondent, you keep a safe distance.

But your relationship can't survive your distance. Your spouse will be reluctant to talk to you about her longing for closeness, fearing more distance.

To break this pattern, you need to know who you are and accept yourself so that you can share yourself freely with your wife. You may need a counselor to help break down the protective barriers surrounding your heart. Then you'll be able to let your wife get close—and allow yourself to get close to her.

#16: The Inhibited Lover

A man can be inhibited about many things—talking about sex, sharing his body, responding sexually, communicating his feelings, being touched, having his sexual parts fondled, making noise, touching his wife's genitals, enjoying her lubrication, or expressing his needs and desires.

If you're an inhibited lover, your wife knows it. She probably doesn't know how to talk to you about your inhibitions and help you past them, though.

You can overcome the restrictions your inhibitions place on the two of you. With your wife, define your inhibitions very specifically. Write them on one side of a piece of paper. On the other side, write what total freedom from your inhibitions would be like.

Then break down in small steps the actions you would take to get from where you are to total freedom with your wife.

#17: The Power-Needy Lover

The power-needy lover wants to dominate. He can't respond when he's not feeling more powerful than his wife.

When she pursues, he rejects. He needs her to give in to his requests for sexual acts that he knows are difficult for her—or at a time that's inconvenient. He sets up a power struggle that he must win.

If this describes you, it's likely that you had power struggles with both parents. Your mother may have dominated and controlled or not been there for you. Your father probably controlled with his physical prowess, perhaps even beating and shaming you.

If you get anxious or upset when you don't have the power, try talking to the little boy in you. Let him know he no longer needs to protect himself against Mom's or Dad's control. You have a wife who can be your companion if you allow her equality with you.

To break your need for power, you may need professional help to understand how you relate to women, to identify your behavioral patterns with your wife, and to counteract both. Action probably will precede feelings. Change will happen as a result of your choice to change.

As you relinquish power, your need for it will diminish. Gradually you'll be able to feel comfortable even when you're not the "power person."

#18: The Disinterested Lover

Guys are supposedly always eager for sex. When a man lacks interest, he may feel unmanly.

It's more common than most people believe for men to struggle with low sexual desire. When it happens, it's also troubling to the wife, who wants to be desired and fulfilled.

There can be many causes for low sexual desire. The naive lover, the bored lover, the insecure lover, and the avoidant lover all have their reasons. So do victims of sexual abuse or trauma; those raised in a rigidly antisexual environment or by a controlling and dominant mother who demeaned men; and those who struggle with an addiction, homosexual fantasies, or other desires that interfere with a desire for one's wife.

Circumstances can also temporarily block your sexual appetite. Preoccupation with job stress, children, or finances could get in the way. Depression, anxiety, or phobias may hinder, especially if they're sexual phobias. Illness, alcohol, prescription drugs, or hormonal disruptions may be physical causes. Relationship conflicts in your marriage can halt your desire. When these problems are dealt with, desire usually returns.

If your lack of desire is due to feelings of sexual inadequacy or deeper emotional issues or trauma, we suggest sexual therapy and psychotherapy. If yours is a relationship issue, marital therapy is needed. A physician can help you deal with physical causes.

Help is available. Your biggest hurdle won't be finding it; it will be your disinterest in doing what's necessary to change.

#19: The Hasty Lover

The man who rushes sex may be insecure, anxious, goal-oriented, or not in control of his ejaculation. He may think of himself as the seven-minute wonder; his wife may think of him as selfish.

If ejaculatory control is your struggle, you're not alone. Of the couples who attend our sexual enhancement seminars, one-third to one-half of the men want to learn how to last longer.

The man who lacks this kind of control ejaculates during preliminary play or within seconds or a few minutes after entry. His wife has no time to respond.

If this is your problem, it may be a habit you learned during adolescent masturbation. Or perhaps you don't know how to pay attention to your arousal level so that you can control it before you get to the point of ejaculation.

You can learn control in this area. Give yourself a couple of months to follow the steps outlined in one of the books available on the subject, such as our own *Restoring the Pleasure* (Word, 1993). That book, and others, explain how to condition your body to extend the length of preorgasmic arousal for longer and longer periods of time.

If you need the counsel of a therapist in this process, don't be afraid to get it. You'll discover greater passion, intensity, and sexual fulfillment as you last longer. You may even go from seven-minute wonder to marathon man!

#20: The Anxious Lover

Anxiety interferes with pleasure and functioning. A man's self-consciousness, watchfulness, monitoring, or spectatoring can keep him from carrying out the sexual act because of his difficulty getting or maintaining an erection.

Anxiety can cause erectile dysfunction in much the same way that it can cause insomnia. You can't just decide to fall asleep at a given moment; given the right conditions, you'll doze off when you're tired. If you concentrate on trying to get an erection, you'll probably keep it from happening. But if you provide the right conditions and are aroused, an erection will occur naturally.

If you're having erectile difficulty, make sure a physical problem isn't causing it. You may need to have an exam that tests penile blood pressure, nighttime erections, hormonal levels, and medication side effects.

If these aren't the cause, you may be an anxious lover. Learn to distract from focusing on performance and refocus on delightful, pleasurable, skin-to-skin contact.

It may help to temporarily rule out intercourse. Your wife must learn to enjoy your body and allow you to enjoy hers without demand for response. You also need to be free to tell your wife when you're anxious.

If a self-help approach is not enough, you may need a sexual therapist. It's worth the effort. You can learn to enjoy sex without anxiety.

#21: The Addicted Lover

If sex controls you, you're sexually addicted. You depend on sexual gratification to feel good and survive. Your sexual behavior, which is connected with anxiety and guilt, is a compulsion.

Your behavior probably has a cycle that begins with preoccupation. Your desire to act builds until you begin a ritual. Your ritual may include rationalizations—telling yourself your actions will not hurt anyone, no one will know, you deserve it, your wife is not meeting your needs, or "good" will come from what you intend to do. You disconnect from your typical way of thinking; you zone out.

Then you act. This might include viewing pornography on the Internet or videos or cable TV, visiting a massage parlor, propositioning a prostitute, having an affair, peeping, cross-dressing, molesting, masturbating, or demanding certain sexual activities with your wife.

Whatever the behavior, it virtually always includes sexual release. With the release comes relief—then despair and remorse, followed by the resolve never to act again. The resolve lasts only so long before the cycle starts again. It may be a pattern you repeat several times a day or several times a year.

You know whether you're addicted. Your wife probably knows, too, even if she hasn't been fully able to admit it to herself.

If you're an addicted lover, your behavior is destroying you and your marital relationship. You're choosing sex in some other form over your wife, violating 1 Corinthians 7:3-5. You're not fulfilling your sexual duty to your wife and giving her authority over your body.

Help is available, and help you will need. Books like Dr. Patrick Carnes' *Out of the Shadows: Understanding Sexual Addiction* (Hazelden Information Education, 2001) and Mark R. Laaser's *Faithful and True* (Zondervan, 1996) are a good place to start. Counseling and commitment to a 12-step program will be necessary.

To get and keep control of your behavior, you must face the fact that you're addicted. You must admit that you'll always need help to stay in control, and accept that you require God's forgiveness and power, as well as accountability to others, to conquer your obsession.

WHEN HERS DOESN'T WORK

When sex isn't working, but you don't see yourself on the previous list, what should you do?

> You may not be responsible for sex not working for your wife, but you may be vital to the solution.

What if your wife is struggling in some area of sexual adjustment or fulfillment? What if she isn't interested—or when she is, nothing happens? What if sex always hurts her?

If you've taken care of your sexual issues, you aren't responsible for the fact that your wife's body isn't working. But you may be part of the solution.

Her Lack of Interest

The most likely reason a woman isn't interested in sex: She associates it with emotional pain, trauma, disappointment, or violation. She may have been exposed to pornography, sexual touching, or other childhood sexual abuse; she may have undergone a traumatic medical genital procedure as a child or adult; or she may have been sexually assaulted in adulthood.

Probably the second most common reason for a lack of desire is a husband who persistently pursues sex. If that's been true for you, it will take time for her to be aware of her own sexuality once you've backed off.

The third, and perhaps most tenacious, reason for disinterest is being the product of an alcoholic home—especially an alcoholic father. The daughter of an alcoholic tends to resist until she becomes physically aroused; then she can be very responsive and have an orgasm, but afterward will quickly shut off interest. She knows how to be out of control, but hates the out-of-control feeling that reminds her of her alcoholic home.

> **Your ability to care for your wife is the start to a positive association between you and her sexual response; sexual interest will follow.**

A woman may lack interest in sex for other reasons—feeling uncared for, seeing sex as a mechanical event to give the man his release, believing pleasure is sinful, or having never heard a positive message about sex within marriage. And as with men, life and relationship stresses, physical and emotional issues, and medications can also zap sexual urges.

Whatever the cause of your wife's disinterest, you can be a major force in the solution. Your sensitivity will be a huge start. Badgering or forcing or cajoling must stop. "Get with her" for her sake, not to get what you want, and she will open up to you. Encourage her to get counseling if she needs it, and cooperate in the process.

As she feels your care, your wife's negative association with sex can become positive. When her sexual responsiveness is linked with feeling heard and understood rather than with pain, pursuit, or trauma, her desire will build.

Her Difficulty with Arousal

Apart from the impact of hormonal changes, a woman rarely has difficulty with arousal responses like vaginal lubrication and nipple erection. Often, however, she's not aware of these reactions; her emotions don't keep up with her body.

The woman who doesn't feel sexual arousal is usually preoccupied with keeping her husband happy or trying to respond for him. She hasn't learned to get in tune with her sexual desires and needs.

Your wife may need permission to go after sex for her own pleasure. You can free her to do that. Encourage her to go with her inner urges rather than focusing on you. Let her know that as long as she's happy, you're happy. She doesn't need to respond or perform for you.

You may need to slow down in order to focus on pleasure rather than results. She'll probably discover sexual potential just waiting to be expressed. Remember, you get the response when you stop trying for it. Enjoy the delightful experience of working on this project together.

Her Difficulty with Orgasm

How would you feel if you rarely or never ejaculated? Just as there's a buildup of sperm and seminal fluid for the man, the arousal process causes the woman to become engorged and physically ready for the orgasmic response. If orgasm doesn't occur, over time she slows herself down so that she gets less and less aroused and eventually doesn't want sex.

> **She has the lead role; you are the supporting actor. Maximize her potential without placing any pressure to perform.**

How can you help? Accept that her orgasm won't make you the lover of all lovers. You're not responsible to give her an orgasm, and she's not responsible to have one for you.

The urge to be orgasmic can come only from her. You can free her so that she doesn't need to have an orgasm for you, but knows you'll participate in whatever way you can to allow her the pleasure she desires.

Since she'll never have an orgasm as an act of the will, encourage her to stop trying—and stop trying to give her one. Enjoy her body for your pleasure rather than for its response; let her know your delight with the person she is. Actively enjoying your body will distract her from self-consciousness and jump-start her body's natural, involuntary responses.

Invite her to share with you what her body hungers for. If she doesn't know, experiment together. Try different types of touch on various areas of her body; let her tell you how each touch feels, not the response it produces.

Accept that she's the authority on her body. What works for one woman may not for another. Think of yourself as a supporting actor in a movie; she's the star. Your role is to do all you can to back her up, to bring her to the place where her sexual potential can be realized.

Her Pain Interrupts Pleasure

Sex was designed to be an enjoyable experience. It wasn't meant to hurt.

When sex is painful for a woman, a physician may have trouble locating the source of the pain. Because her genitals look normal upon examination, the woman may get the message, directly or indirectly, that the pain is all in her head.

Our response is, "No, it's in her vagina!" After 20 years of treating women who experience painful intercourse, we've never seen a woman who created or imagined her pain.

Can pain be due to stress? Absolutely. But most often, pain is due to a tight muscle that resulted from trauma or infection or irritation, or a tear, or some other physical condition. Even if the pain is caused by anxiety, it still hurts. It still requires physical intervention.

What can you do? Take her pain seriously. Don't continue the painful experiences.

Help her identify and isolate the nature of her pain. Exactly *when* in the experience does the pain occur? Pinpoint *where* the pain is felt. Is it on the outer edge of the vagina, just inside the opening, around the muscle that controls the opening of the vagina, or deep within? Is it a spot or an area? *What* type of pain is it? Stinging, stabbing, or a general irritation?

Once your wife can answer these questions, she can help her physician to be more effective in diagnosis and treatment. If her doctor is unwilling or unable to identify the source of the pain, she should keep looking. She might need to find a vulvar pain specialist, who may have specialized in both gynecology and urology.

> **Pain always needs to be taken seriously and at face value.**

Until your wife's pain is relieved, your sexual life won't be satisfying and fulfilling. She needs you as her ally, reassuring her that there is always an answer, and there is always somebody who can help.

BE THE LOVER OF YOUR WIFE

What kind of lover do you want to be to your wife?

Maybe you saw yourself in bits and pieces of those 21 descriptions of dysfunctional lovers. We hope you're thinking of ways to begin changing that.

Your body isn't your own; it's hers. As you learn to be a giving and serving lover, you'll bring greater love, passion, and intimacy to your marriage. You'll counter the wifely disillusionment that so often results when a husband won't get beyond himself and into his wife's world.

Whether it's some part of you or some part of her that's not working, defining the issues and applying the solutions will bring the two of you closer together. Your bonus will be the delight of a full, unencumbered sexual life—or to put it another way, a lot more fun in bed with your wife.

CHAPTER EIGHT

AFFAIR PROOF YOUR MARRIAGE

Protecting your marriage may seem unnecessary. You and your wife may be strongly committed to each other and to God; infidelity isn't an option. Won't your love for each other keep you from being attracted to someone else?

Consider the story of Sam and Jenny.

They'd been married for 12 years. They viewed their relationship as solid. Their only tension was around sex: Jenny's lack of interest really bothered Sam, while she often felt her only value to Sam was sexual.

Their children were both in school, so Jenny decided to go back to work part time as an accountant for a large firm. When she did, she met Bill.

He was the accountant who worked next to her. Bill had finished divorce proceedings with his wife two months before. He started to ask Jenny questions about how to handle issues with his children; Jenny found herself sharing more and more with him.

One day it hit her: *Bill cares about me as a person. He's not just interested in my body.*

That's probably when the affair started.

UNDERSTANDING YOUR VULNERABILITY

Even though you may take seriously the Bible's instructions to become one flesh as husband and wife and not allow the marriage bed to be defiled, you're human.

In *Marriage Partnership* magazine, Harold B. Smith interviewed men about their struggles in this area:

> DAN: The idea of beautiful women who always want you, who are always inviting, who aren't angry with you and whom you won't have to deal with on an emotional level—that's very appealing. And I carried that fantasy into our marriage.
>
> MIKE: I guess my fantasy is to have a woman who wants me so badly she can't keep her hands off me. But that's a fantasy because, one, my wife's not geared that way—although she's geared enough that way that I'm still hoping! And two, I feel that the initiating is my responsibility. I need to court her, to let her know she's desirable to me, to let her know I would love to make love to her. And I think she wants that.
>
> KENT: I was surprised to find out that lust doesn't stop with marriage. If anything, it grows because now you have someone to have sex with and the sensual world around you is saying, "Try this. And now try this!" You somehow think that all of the media images of sexuality should be experienced in your own love life.[1]

When the Grass Looks Greener

Once you live with someone day after day, year after year, you tend to see faults. The very characteristics that once intrigued you now irritate.

When Jenny seemed hard to get sexually, for example, Sam was challenged to conquer. Initially, when he was so responsive to her body, Jenny responded with excitement. But no more.

Neither Jenny nor Sam contemplated this fact: Newness excites, and it hides flaws.

Situations Provide Opportunities

Feelings toward a person of the opposite sex may develop when you're in frequent or ongoing contact with him or her. Attraction and attachment have the opportunity to grow. It can happen between fellow workers, close friends, or neighbors. It can seem so natural, almost irresistible, and so right!

On the other hand, you can work with some people closely for years, highly respect them, even like them—but never find yourself attracted to them. That's why it's so important to know yourself and the type of person who triggers your vulnerability.

> **Know yourself, and know your vulnerability.**

Situational attractions happen to some more than others. If you or your wife tends to be vulnerable in this area, be vigilant to safeguard your home fort.

What makes some people more prone to affairs is not totally understood. Some seem to be scanners looking for opportunities; others seem to give off vibes that attract.

Why feelings happen between two people and not between others is also not clear. Some factors—body scent and type, and emotional and intellectual type—seem to make a difference. You and your wife should develop an understanding of the categories that tend to attract each of you, and be accountable to each other regarding individuals who are "your type."

According to Harville Hendrix in *Getting the Love You Want,* you're more likely to attach to someone you feel might give you the parental love or affirmation you never received. Being attracted to someone may have to do with finding your parent in that person.[2]

Life Change Increases Vulnerability

Any change in life, positive or negative, is a stress in the sense that it jars loose your sense of security. The intensity of life change will determine how susceptible you are to an outside attachment.

> **Desiring change at home may also increase the likelihood of responding to an attraction.**

That was the case with Jenny. After being a stay-at-home mom for 12 years, she got a new job. Her eagerness to do well in the workplace, dressing for work, interacting daily with adults—all were conditions of change that increased her vulnerability.

Jenny's response to Bill was heightened by the fact that she wanted Sam to share with her and listen to her as Bill did. Even though she never thought, *If I have an affair with Bill, I'll get Sam's attention on me and off sex and get him to understand what I need from him,* that was what happened.

Insecurity Seeks Validation

Imagine that you're not very sure of yourself. Growing up, you had to perform to get your mother's love or attention. Now your wife doesn't seem to affirm you, either. Sometimes it seems all she gives you is a list of things to do or ways in which she'd like you to be different.

You go to work. Your female co-worker thinks you're the best at what you do.

What happens when she looks into your eyes and says, "You're something else"?

Or imagine that your wife has never felt good about herself. When other girls were maturing physically, she was still flat-chested; she never did develop as fully as she wanted to. That's never bothered you, but your words don't seem to make a difference. Her discomfort with her body gets in the way of wanting and enjoying sex with you.

What happens when the guy next door expresses his attraction to her?

Addictive Tendencies Hook

The adrenaline rush of doing something wrong may trigger passion and sexual excitement.

If you tend to associate risk and guilt with sex, it may have begun with masturbation or doing more with your girlfriend than you thought was right. When sexual feelings first emerge in association with an activity believed to be illicit, sex may be experienced as feeling good when it's wrong—and lack intensity in the context of marriage, where it's considered right.

> If sex is good only when it's wrong, it can never be great when it's right.

We've found that sexual patterns are easily conditioned. The activity or event that evokes sexual feelings and responses for the first time can become the condition needed for all future sexual excitement and response.

That's one reason we're so adamant that parents teach their children to affirm sexual feelings and take responsibility for their actions. Children must know that God designed their genitals with wonderful sexual feelings and responses, and that He designed sexual union and pleasure as an expected part of the marital relationship. Teaching against touching genitals, for example, leads to inauthentic guilt and the connection of good, God-given sexual feelings with doing wrong.

A person who associates sex with risk and guilt will come to marriage unable to enjoy the full potential of sex when it's right—and be more vulnerable to going for sex when it's wrong.

An Unhappy Marriage Provides an Excuse

No marriage is without some discontent. No spouse can meet all of a person's needs.

Still, if you fall short on many of Dr. Neil Clark Warren's 10 love secrets for a lasting marriage detailed in *Learning to Live with the Love of Your Life . . . and Loving It!*, you're at risk for an affair.[3]

If you don't keep your emotional marital bank account full as Gary Smalley recommends in his chapter on marriage in *Go the Distance: The Making of a Promise Keeper*, you're more vulnerable to infidelity.[4]

If you don't manage the ratio of five positives to one negative that Dr. John Gottman has found essential to marriages that last (described in *Why Marriages Succeed or Fail*), you're in danger of unfaithfulness.[5]

Unhappy marriages don't excuse affairs—except in the minds of those who use them as rationalizations.

PREVENT AN AFFAIR

Finding intimacy outside marriage may be tempting when life at home gets boring, or you feel you're giving more than you're getting. But it's not only wrong—it's messy.

Keeping your marriage free of infidelity is a commitment you can make. Keeping that commitment will be well worth your effort.

No One Is Exempt

First, face reality and accept your vulnerability. You may not be looking to greener grass, be attracted to a co-worker or neighbor, face any change or want to effect change in your marriage, or be insecure or addictive. You may be delighted with your wife and she with you. But you are not exempt from temptation. You are human.

> **Marital love is challenged when temptation tests your belief that love will prevent an affair.**

The Bible's instruction is clear: We are to choose one spouse and commit to live faithfully with him or her for the rest of our lives. It doesn't say that because we make that choice, we won't be attracted to others. We are responsive sexual beings, and that responsiveness is not selective.

When you aren't protecting your marriage, you may be taken by surprise. Feelings for someone else can seem to zap you out of nowhere, or build gradually without your realizing how it happened.

It has nothing to do with love, but infatuation can seem even more intense.

This may never happen to you. Or it may happen once or twice in your lifetime. If and when it does, your assumption that love alone would protect you will cause you to question that love.

A Strong Marriage Is a Protective Shield

Strong marriages tend to repel unfaithfulness. But strong marriages don't just happen. Here are six ways to build the kind of relationship that protects against infidelity.

1. *Invest time and energy.* Many times a man or woman will complain about a marriage, yet will invest little in improving it. When an extramarital attraction beckons, the same person makes a huge effort to make the new connection work.

If that much commitment was put into the marriage, *Hot Monogamy* (the title of a book by therapist Patricia Love[6]) would be inevitable. As we've said before, invest at least fifteen minutes per day, one evening per week, one day per month, and one weekend per season. This is the Penner formula for a lasting marriage.

2. *Understand and accept differences.* Even though the feminine uniqueness of your wife probably attracted you to her, you may often feel the frustration of Professor Henry Higgins in *My Fair Lady*: "Why can't a woman be more like a man?"

Don't expect your wife to become more like you. And remember that differences can work for you rather than against you when you understand and accept them.

3. *Pursue common interests.* You and your wife may have lost track of common dreams. What did you enjoy doing when you dated? What did you anticipate when you planned your mar-

riage? What new ideas have you had since? Have you listened to her thoughts and goals?

4. *Build togetherness.* We often get letters and calls from women who are frustrated with their husbands' lack of spiritual and emotional connection with them. We recommend taking 15 minutes per day maintaining that connection. If you'll do that—talking, reading the Bible, and praying with your wife —she'll be more enthusiastic in bed and your relationship will be strengthened.

5. *Have fun and play together.* Let the child in you play with the child in her. Be careful about teasing, though. Many children are raised with hurtful teasing that they bring into marriage and use to hurt each other.

Delight in each other. For more ideas on having fun, see Chapter 11.

6. *Renew your commitment to each other.* As 1 Corinthians 13 makes clear, love isn't a feeling; it's a commitment to behave lovingly toward each other. It's nurtured by the demonstration of respect, tenderness, and thoughtfulness. It's damaged by sarcasm, criticism, neglect, and disregard. So honor your commitment by:

- never giving up
- caring more for each other than for self
- not wanting what you don't have
- not strutting
- not having a swelled head
- not forcing yourself on your wife
- not always thinking about "me first"
- not flying off the handle
- not keeping score of the wrongdoing of your wife
- not reveling when your wife is groveling

- taking pleasure in the flowering of the truth
- putting up with anything
- trusting God always (adapted from 1 Corinthians 13, *The Message*).

A Pure Mind Controls Actions

Proverbs 23:7 declares, "For as he thinks in his heart, so is he."

In psychology, we talk about mental rehearsal. For example, a speaker can rehearse his fear of stumbling when he speaks and be more likely to actually stumble—or he can deal with his fear of stumbling by picturing himself in the speaking situation and performing smoothly. What he rehearses mentally will affect the outcome of his actual presentation.

You can heighten the danger of an affair by rehearsing and nurturing fantasies of unfaithfulness. When they move from fleeting thoughts to lust, they move from temptation to the sin of committing adultery in your heart (see Matthew 5:28).

To help protect yourself against an affair, fill your mind with images of loving, fun, fantastic sex with your wife. Free your mind of input that encourages adultery—whether it's from Internet sites, magazines, videos, movies, or television programs. Study positive, biblical messages about sexuality. Read the Song of Solomon with your wife.

Speedy Exits Prevent Disaster

What's your plan to flee the temptation of an affair?

Have a plan of action and rehearse it mentally. Discuss with your wife what each of you would do if you found yourself connecting with someone else. When temptation comes, take prompt, decisive action:

1. Tell someone other than the person to whom you're attracted. If your relationship can handle it, tell your spouse.
2. Be accountable to someone other than, or in addition to, your spouse.
3. Remove yourself from contact with the person who attracts you. That may even mean changing jobs.
4. Make a plan to counter temptation should you have accidental contact with the person.
5. Rehearse #4 frequently.
6. Reject fantasies that are nurturing the temptation.
7. Pour yourself into your marriage, reading God's Word, and prayer.

Don't Let It Happen to You

Practicing faithfulness in your mind and actions will bring lasting joy to you as a person—and to your relationship with your wife.

Drink water from your own cistern, and fresh water from your own well. Should your springs be dispersed abroad, streams of water in the streets? Let them be yours alone, and not for strangers with you (Proverbs 5:15).

CHAPTER NINE

HAVE AN ADVENTURE WITH YOUR WIFE

L ooking for some sexual spark in your life? The best place to look is at home.

Dan and Kate enjoyed their sexual relationship and had the qualities of a great marriage. But with both working and investing in the active lives of their three children, sex wasn't happening as often as they liked.

One day, Dan was meeting with an attractive female client. He found himself imagining pursuing her. He became alarmed.

Then he thought, *Why not do that with Kate?*

That thought led to pursuing an adventure with his wife.

WHY AN ADVENTURE?

We're not encouraging you to fantasize about being unfaithful, or to act out an illicit affair to "spice up" your sex life. We're encouraging an adventure as yourselves, something more than just planning a time away. Special times away for a couple are vital to keeping a relationship nurtured, but an adventure with your wife is something only monogamy can bring.

The Adrenaline Hook

Adrenaline is a hormone released in the body in reaction to stress and intense emotions. Its revitalizing quality can hook individuals into having an affair.

Fortunately, having an affair isn't the only way to experience an adrenaline rush. An erotic adventure with your wife can provide it, too.

To stay alive and vibrant, your marriage needs intensity. Passion will die without expression of a whole range of powerful emotions. The bond of opening yourselves to each other without inhibition by sharing an adventure will keep enough adrenaline coursing through your blood to counteract the "take each other for granted" attitude of a long-term committed relationship.

> **Passion will die without expression of a whole range of powerful emotions.**

The Power of Newness

In an affair, everything is new. The two people are new to each other. They discover their bodies, emotions, and intellects—albeit in the wrong context. Irritations and disappointments haven't surfaced yet. There are no responsibilities, crises, or burdens to manage.

How can that anticipation and discovery happen between two married people who know each other intimately? How can it happen when they have to work to pay the mortgage, unclog the shower drain, take care of their vomiting child in the middle of the night, and try to ignore each other's annoying habits?

Creating the newness dimension in your marriage will be more difficult than squeezing out a little adrenaline. But you can do it! Here are three suggestions.

1. *Be a new you.* You can start with a makeover. Become a new man by eliminating habits that your wife has complained about.

If it bugs her when you pick your face, scalp, or nose, stop!

If she's asked you to empathize with and support her rather than offering solutions when she's distressed, do it!

It she's told you to hang up your clean clothes and put your dirty ones in the hamper, start now!

If you used to dress nicely when you were courting her, do it again!

One couple we worked with was separated. They were trying to resolve their issues and get reconnected. They liked to bike together, but she was disgusted by how he dressed when he biked.

One day he called on his cell phone, asking her to meet him.

"Where are you?" she asked.

He told her to look across the street. There were a number of bikers. Finally she noticed a guy in a totally new biking outfit and realized it was her husband. She not only started to laugh, but also rushed out to meet him.

There are many ways to create a new you. Even small additions or corrections will make a difference.

2. *Find a new setting.* It might be a hotel, motel, resort, recreational vehicle, houseboat, train, or campground. Your home could be the location for an erotic adventure with your wife, but you'll

have to invest time and energy to create a new setting within the familiar space.

Whatever location you choose, make it different from what the two of you are used to.

3. *Discover a new experience.* It's natural to repeat the same sexual experience over and over again. But there's so much wasted potential in marriages, so many wonderfully new moments to discover. We're sometimes amazed that after 40 years of marriage, we can find something totally new about one of us that brings a whole new awareness to our enjoyment of each other sexually.

> There's so much wasted potential in marriages; there's so much newness waiting to be discovered.

You may feel self-conscious or silly behaving or dressing differently from the way you usually do. Nudge yourself a little. If finding a new setting and creating a new experience seem impossible, you might use a book of ideas.

If the adventure isn't intended as a surprise, include her in the fun of planning. Erotic adventures can evolve as a mutual effort, not just as one spouse pursues the other.

Reluctant as you may be to venture beyond the safe bounds of your current habits, you'll experience fresh vitality with your wife as you strive to capture her heart anew.

HOW DOES AN ADVENTURE LOOK?

When the passion of a relationship begins to slip, the remedy is willingness to risk—to live life with emotional vulnerability and openness, to look for newness, to do the unexpected.

Imagine for a moment the risks Dan would have taken if he'd pursued his client rather than his wife. He would have had to risk letting her know of his attraction to her without knowing whether she was attracted to him. He might have made the initial move and followed up with body language, looks, telephone calls, and eventually action.

Dan let himself do just that—but with Kate, his wife. He called and talked with her. He expressed interest in her and what was happening in her day and how impressed he was with how she'd handled a project she was working on. He wooed her.

At first Kate questioned his motives, but he kept stating his positive thoughts and affections toward her. He invited her to lunch to talk about some decisions they needed to make—probably the excuse he would have used to initiate a lunch appointment with his client.

Curious, Kate accepted. That was the beginning of that couple's revitalizing sexual adventure.

Are you willing to make the move on your wife and take the risks that would involve? You might get rejected. Dan could have been. But the risk unleashed the adrenaline and added a whole new dimension to his and Kate's sex life.

Getting to know someone is a risk, too. You may think you know everything about your wife, but many little details are yet to be revealed. Those discoveries can bring spark to a marriage. The passion you desire can be resurrected after having been buried for years.

Getting to know your wife may seem difficult, assuming you already feel attached to and comfortable with her. You may have to recall how you won her trust and friendship initially. Winning her anew is likely to stir up romance for both of you.

You may feel awkward if you haven't behaved in winsome ways with your wife in a long time. But the risk of trying some of those old courting behaviors can raise adrenaline levels and vitality, too.

Five Keys to Adventure

Here are five ingredients to make your sexual adventure with your wife a success:

1. *Share a secret.* A secret between two people can be a cord that ties them together. Creating a secret adventure with your wife will get some adrenaline flowing and newness happening.

It's great for a husband and wife to have secrets—information and experiences they've shared that no one else in the world, not even their therapist, knows.

Secrets bind. So why not bind the two of you more intimately?

2. *Plan ahead.* You can make beautiful music in your marriage by orchestrating an erotic adventure that has just the right timing, intensity, balance, rhythm, crescendos, and decrescendos. You must know what each of you likes and dislikes and how you respond to various situations. Then you can plan.

When Dan met Kate for lunch, he had the entire afternoon mapped. He knew she would respond positively to a surprise, so without her knowledge he'd arranged for after-school child care, packed appropriate clothing, reserved a private booth at a new restaurant, and checked out their hotel room to make certain it had all the trappings they'd enjoy in their afternoon rendezvous.

3. *Be on your best behavior.* By the time you've invested this much in your adventure with your wife, you'll be highly motivated to be on your best behavior.

Bringing your best will enhance the event. Keep in mind that it usually takes careful planning to show your best to the one you love most deeply.

4. *Commit time and energy.* We're always amazed to discover how many hours and how much effort very busy individuals can waste on an affair. You may think you don't have time or energy for an adventure with your wife. But if you want intensity in your intimacy, be willing to invest yourself. You'll get results.

5. *Entice your spouse.* Do you find the lively, enthusiastic woman you married to be rather mundane now? You can dazzle her and awaken her sexual vibrancy. If you're fortunate enough to be married to a woman who's kept her passion and even seen it blossom, she'll become even more alive in response to your enticement.

To lure a woman, you must first clear out past hurts and resentments. Apologize as needed.

If your wife feels cared for, understood, and validated by you, you'll get a spirited and positive response. You might precede enticement with a check-in talk on how she's feeling about the two of you. Make certain you're on good terms.

King Solomon is an excellent example of an enticer. He adored, praised, and delighted in his wife. She responded by inviting him to enjoy her body. Go for it!

GATEWAY TO ADVENTURE

Dr. Elaine Hatfield, a psychologist specializing in research on love, reports that passionate love dwindles after the first six to thirty months in a relationship. But we're convinced that erotic decline isn't a necessary consequence of longtime married relationships.

Passion may change from the initial newness to deeper fulfillment, but it's a lifelong possibility.

Adding adventure to the deep love and secure commitment of marriage is the best way to develop a lifelong, generous, playful, mature sexual vibrancy. True passion is being erotic with someone you know intimately and love and desire so much that you continue to be married.

So plan that erotic adventure with your wife this week!

Let your fountain be blessed, and rejoice in the wife of your youth. As a loving hind and a graceful doe, let her breasts satisfy you at all times; be exhilarated always with her love (Proverbs 5:18-19).

CHAPTER TEN

THE WORKING SIDE OF SEX

S ex is to be fun!

That fact is reflected in the pleasure it brings, the charge of the passion, the sensations of building arousal, and the release of orgasm. There's deep satisfaction in those primitive delights, and in connecting at your core with the person you love enough to have committed your life to.

Sex is also serious and takes work.

Spiritually, sex between a husband and wife symbolizes the most important relationship, the one between Christ and His people. Sex reflects the depth of commitment that grows in a relationship. It asks complete abandonment and vulnerability. Serious feelings get stirred up in the process of being sexual; sexual rights within marriage demand serious respect; and sexual responsibility is a serious requirement of every believer.

So sex has both a fun side and a serious side. And when it comes to great sex in marriage, serious work is often a prerequisite to fun. In this chapter we'll start with the work.

TEN GOOD WAYS TO WORK AT SEX

Way #1: Think

Here are some questions to ask yourself:

What kind of lover are you, and what kind would you like to be?

How has your sexual life progressed over the years?

What are the messages you've heard from your wife about sex?

What sexual tension has there been between the two of you?

What's your wife's attitude about your sexual relationship?

What are the sexual issues you think about?

You probably think about your financial future. You cogitate about your career. If you're a parent, you consider how you're doing in raising your children and what you foresee in their futures. Why not do the same with your sexual life?

Way #2: Plan

Your planning will reflect your thinking. It will also involve your wife.

> **Plans need to bring about the fulfillment of mutual dreams, not private dreams that induce pressure or demand.**

You may never have thought of having sexual goals. They can be helpful if they're not performance goals but long-term dreams. They need to be behaviors you can control, not involuntary bodily responses.

Here are some examples:

- working on getting control of premature ejaculation during the next six months

- allowing longer periods of pleasure and increased intensity for your wife (not arousal and orgasm, which are involuntary responses)
- taking turns preparing the setting for your sexual times, to create a more interesting atmosphere
- reading a chapter of a book like this to each other each week
- setting aside an hour at bedtime several nights a week to just enjoy each other's bodies with no demand for arousal or release
- building a 15-minute connecting and kissing time into your daily routine
- trying methods of birth control that are less interruptive than your current method.

Whatever your goals, pursue them together—and without placing demand or pressure on each other.

Way #3: Schedule

Schedule sex? How boring!

But think about it. Was dating boring? Didn't you schedule your dates? Did the scheduling interfere with your ability to become aroused and wish you could have sex?

We remember parking at the conclusion of a scheduled date and kissing and wanting so much to do more that it practically drove us crazy. Scheduling increases anticipation, and anticipation sparks passion.

> Spontaneity can work if initiated by the woman. A turned-on woman is usually a turn-on to a man; a turned-on man is frequently a demand to a woman.

You can look forward to your times together and picture how you'd like them to be. Try it. You'll like it!

Spontaneity may be great, but it's not a necessary ingredient for an exciting sexual life. For most couples, scheduled spontaneity works best.

In your scheduled times, you're not scheduling intercourse, arousal, or release. They're not necessary ingredients of every great and passionate time together in marriage.

Some couples shun scheduling because they think they should come to their sexual times already interested or aroused. That's a myth. You're scheduling time to be together that may or may not grow into a full sexual experience. In contrast to your dating days, you now have the freedom to do as much or as little as each of you desires in the moment. You'll be amazed at how quickly you can get interested if the two of you spend a little time together and start behaving in sexual ways.

You may be an exception to our scheduling recommendation. If you're together as much as both of you want to be, your sexual life is full and vibrant and mutually satisfying, and you're not scheduling, more power to you. Continue to enjoy and feel fortunate.

For the other 99 out of 100 of you, be like one couple we know, Sue and Bob. Get out your calendars every Sunday night and plan for the week ahead. And be sure to practice the habit of quickly rescheduling when you cancel a prearranged time.

Way #4: Shop
What does shopping have to do with sex? Quite a lot!

Shopping with your wife in mind is one way to tell her you care. The size of the gift or purchase is insignificant. She doesn't need a new Mercedes to feel that you love her. She needs to know you were thinking of her.

If she broke a lace on her tennis shoes, pick up a pair to save her a trip. That little purchase can be as valuable as a new piece of jewelry. It says, "I'm thinking about you and want to serve you."

Shopping for items related to your sex life can be fun, too. Pick up your favorite lubricant at the drugstore, buy scented candles to put by the bed, get softer sheets, or buy a book that offers sound sexual advice. Be aware, though, that she may consider a book on sex as a demand. If she hasn't read the last three you bought, you probably can count on her not reading the next one, either.

> Shopping can spark sex if it doesn't elicit pressure or attempt to buy sex or love.

You must also know your wife to know if lingerie would be an appropriate choice. Some would see it as a demand.

Shopping together also can be fun, as long as the agenda is mutually satisfying.

Two warnings:

1. You must remember your anniversary, Valentine's Day, her birthday, Christmas, and Mother's Day (if she's a mom).

2. You can't buy sex or love. Your wife must experience purchases as an outgrowth of your care and thoughtfulness.

Way #5: Talk

Men don't want to *talk* about sex; they want to *have* it. Women want to talk about it, have it, talk about it, and have it.

Your wife wants to talk; she wants you to be interested in her. You're probably going to have to do the "talk" part if the "have" part is going to be any good. Every time you move in her direction, both of you benefit. You're happy as she's happy; it's a win-win situation.

Talking during the sexual experience is a personal choice. Some couples like to talk a lot during lovemaking; others make love in total silence and are completely happy.

A woman prefers to have her husband talk about his delight in *her*, not just in her sexual parts. One woman told us how furious she was with her husband for not talking about her as a person, and for referring to her genitals in slang terms. Some women love being earthy during sex, but most find it offensive. Deciding how explicit to be calls on your sensitivity.

Talk during sex about what either of you likes or doesn't like is often best accompanied by showing. If you've talked apart from the sexual experience about your preferences, then during sex you can refer to that conversation in a few words and with a bit of touch.

Talking that analyzes your sex life, vital though it is, should happen apart from the sexual experience itself. It needn't be only about difficulties; it should also be about what excites each of you.

If you find it hard to talk about sex, maybe you don't know what words to use. You feel awkward because you're not quite sure what to call various parts. Maybe you never heard sex talked about in your family or only heard it mentioned crassly in the locker room. Try reading this book aloud with your wife. You'll probably become more comfortable using correct sexual terminology.

Your sexual talk times should have boundaries. Neither of you should refer to how some prior partner behaved sexually, even if you never had sexual intercourse with that person. The reasons for making such comparisons are usually hostile, and hostility never serves either spouse.

Another boundary to respect: Don't criticize things that can't be changed. Her coarse pubic hair is what you got when you married her. Drawing attention to it only creates tension and distance.

The need for couples to talk about sex became clear to us when we did a two-week series called "Pure and Simple Sex" for a Los Angeles TV station. The producers asked people coming out of divorce court, "How much did sex have to do with your divorce?"

Husbands reported that sex had nothing to do with it; wives reported that sex had much to do with it. What clear evidence of how poorly the couples had communicated about their sexual lives—and how essential it is that talking is part of yours.

Way #6: Learn

Learning about sex is a lifelong process. You can still be growing in this area 20, 40, or 60 years into your marriage.

Learn about her body and yours. Tell each other how you feel about your bodies—what you like and don't like. Affirm the positives you feel toward each other's bodies.

Discover together the kind of bodily touching you like, including genital touch. Building familiarity will reduce anxiety and increase pleasure.

Accept the fact that as your wife's body changes, her desires will change. Her body will go through many more fluctuations than yours because of her monthly cycles, possible pregnancy and childbirth, menopause, and perhaps even a hysterectomy. You'll be forever learning.

Way #7: Practice

Practicing naturally follows learning.

You may need to practice ejaculatory control. You may need to practice talking or general caressing or limiting yourself to no genital touch for the first 15 minutes. You may need practice to stimulate her genitally.

Perhaps your wife responds to stimulation of the G-spot, located in the upper inside of the vagina just beyond the vaginal muscle. You may need a lot of practice finding that area and learning to touch it so that it brings pleasure rather than pain.

Kissing may require practice. For some couples, passionate kissing is natural; for many, it's not.

Don't assume that your wife likes the way you kiss. Let her show you what she prefers. You'll probably like what she likes, but she may not like what you like.

We find that when a woman is free to teach her husband how she likes to kiss, he loves it. The opposite is often not true. Once she's shown you, practice daily—even if it's just for 60 seconds. Kissing is a key to keeping sex working!

Way #8: Take Responsibility

Sex works best in a loving relationship if each spouse takes responsibility for himself or herself.

Assume that your spouse doesn't know and can't sense what feels best to you at any given moment. Even after you've taught each other what you like and practiced the basics, only you will feel what your body hungers for. Learn to listen to and communicate that hunger as you respond to what she's telling you about her own.

When you accept responsibility for your sexual desires without demand or violation of the other, you also accept responsibility to enjoy the other's body for your pleasure—counting on the other to let you know if your touch isn't pleasurable. This feedback loop brings the greatest enjoyment for both.

Way #9: Negotiate

You can negotiate differences about sex just as you can in every other area of life. Great sex meets both spouses' needs; it can't be dictated by one person.

Many couples don't think of negotiating about sex. They believe sex is just supposed to "click." But marriage works best in all areas when a couple learns to negotiate.

Compromise is often wise. If one of you likes the sexual experience best in the morning and the other likes it at night, try alternating or meeting at noon. If one of you prefers to make love with all the lights on and the blankets off the bed, while the other likes the dark and a cozy feeling under the blankets, try dim lighting and less covering.

Sometimes compromise seems impossible. For example, one of you may like oral sex while the other is repulsed by it. Respect each other's feelings. Do nothing in violation of or at the expense of either person. In the negotiation process, always go with the most conservative spouse; that way no one will be violated. Accept the fact that you won't always get what you want.

> **Negotiate your differences so that both of you are respected and neither is violated.**

Here's a checklist of common differences between spouses. It reflects personal preferences, not rights or wrongs. Make two photocopies; each of you should complete a copy.

Discuss the results. When you disagree, determine how important that item is to each of you. Add your own unique differences at the end and discuss those, too.

Try looking at this checklist every year on your anniversary. Use it as a tool to help you accept and negotiate your differences.

Common Differences to Be Negotiated

____ I like to initiate.   ____ I like my spouse to initiate.

____ I like making love in .   ____ I like making love at night.
     the morning

____ Direct initiation is   ____ I like subtle initiation.
     the most positive for me.

____ I like to have sex several   ____ Having sex once every week
     times a week.   or two is fine with me.

____ I like long kisses.   ____ I like short kisses.

____ I like wet kisses.   ____ I like dry kisses.

I like to talk a lot   I have little need for talking
____ before making love   ____ before making love
____ while making love   ____ while making love
____ after making love.   ____ after making love.

____ Explicit sexual talk is   ____ I like subtle and indirect
     arousing for me.   sexual talk.

____ I like to get lots of touching.   ____ I don't have much need
                                                to get touching.

___ I like to give lots of touching.___ I don't have much need to
give touching.

___ Direct stimulation is   ___ I like very indirect
most positive for me.   stimulation.

___ I like to make love with   ___ I like the lights off.
the lights on.

___ I like my spouse to have   ___ I'm uncomfortable being
eyes open during lovemaking.   watched by my spouse.

___ I like oral sex when it's the   ___ I don't like oral sex when it's
woman stimulating the man.   the woman stimulating the
man.

___ I like oral sex when it's the   ___ I don't like oral sex when it's
man stimulating the woman.   the man stimulating the
woman.

___ I like our lovemaking to   ___ I like it to be pretty much
be different every time.   the same every time.

___ I look forward to a lot of   ___ I like predictability.
excitement and creativity.

___ I feel a strong connection   ___ I don't sense much connec-
between my sexuality and   tion between the two.
my spirituality.

Way #10: Expect Change

Change is constant. Expect to grow in sexual understanding and experience, and never to reach perfection in either.

Christians are to have a relationship with God that's new every morning. Similarly, you can strive toward deeper love, more intense passion, and closer intimacy with your wife—knowing that you'll always be learning and changing and discovering newness together.

Change counteracts routine. Since routine stifles passion, change is vital to keeping passion in a marriage.

And that's a goal worth working for.

CHAPTER ELEVEN

THE LIGHTER SIDE OF SEX

So much for the serious side of sex.
It's not all work—it's a lot of play, too.

> Enjoy life with the woman whom you love all the days of your
> fleeting life which He has given to you under the sun; for this
> is your reward in life (Ecclesiastes 9:9).

Let's look at some good ways to enjoy this reward from our Creator.

TEN WAYS TO HAVE FUN WITH SEX

Way #1: Laugh

God had quite a sense of humor when He designed sex. Think of what you do in a sexual experience. It's actually pretty hilarious, isn't it?

When sex gets too serious, bring the humorous view of God's design into the bedroom. A little laughter can ease those marital mishaps. An elbow in the ribs or a slip of the penis out of the vagina at the wrong moment can be fun if you laugh together instead of getting angry.

Laughter heals. It relieves tension and brings the two of you together. Silliness can't be planned, but you can allow for it and look for opportunities to let it out.

We've laughed so hard that several times one of us has fallen off the bed. Once, early in our marriage, we shook the bed with our laughter; a vase on the headboard hit Joyce on the head, giving her a real goose egg. We wondered how we'd explain our mishap if she had to go to the emergency room.

One caution: Never laugh at the expense of your spouse. Laughter is fun only if both enjoy it.

Way #2: Experiment

To experiment is to test how something works or discover something new. You can't fail when you experiment because there's no predetermined outcome.

When we work with couples in sexual therapy, they sometimes report discouragement that an exercise "didn't work." Our response is that if they tried it, it worked. Because every assignment is an experiment to learn what each spouse likes, there's no way to fail. There's no prescribed response.

> **You can't fail when you experiment because there's no predetermined outcome.**

To try new ways of sexual interaction, you may need a nudge. If your wife is more of an experimenter than you are, let her lead. If neither of you is apt to be experimental, here are some ideas:

- change who usually initiates
- select a new location
- take turns being active
- start differently from the way you usually do
- caress each other everywhere except breasts or genitals
- use any part of your body except your hands to pleasure your spouse
- choose three objects of different textures (silk, cashmere, etc.) to pleasure the other, starting on the other's back; the one being pleasured guesses what's being used and selects one of the objects for a total body caress
- act out the breathing and sounds of sexual response
- write love letters to each other describing a sexual experience of your choice
- without entry, try putting your bodies in as many positions as you can think of: your wife on top, you on top, sitting, standing, on the bed, on a chair, side by side, legs between, legs around, on the edge of the bed, kneeling beside the bed, spooning (one behind the other), etc. This can be more silly than stimulating, but you may find something you like.

Way #3: Surprise

Surprises thrill some people and immobilize others. If your wife likes surprises, they're a good way to send the message of thoughtfulness.

If your spouse prefers predictability, plan your surprises together. Outline her surprise birthday party with her. Give her gifts from her wish list. Decide in concert on a special evening or sexual time.

If your wife sees surprises as a language of love and you do them well, go for it. You might pack a feather in the luggage to pleasure her with when you arrive at a hotel. Pull a surprise gift from under the bedcovers. Show up early from work with take-out food when you know she's stressed and missing you. When she gets home from work late, run a bubble bath for her, put the kids in bed, and offer to caress her with lotion—without expecting that she'll respond with desire for intercourse.

Most women prefer tender, loving, thoughtful surprises, not the kind that have too much adrenaline connected with them. All surprises must be freely given without demand for response.

Surprises involve risk. Not every one will work, but if you're willing to take a chance, you'll discover what does.

Way #4: Shock

A shock is a *big* surprise.

When we were taping our video series *The Magic and Mystery of Sex* in Cleveland, we asked one couple, John and Becky, what kept their sexual life so vibrant. Becky replied, "A bit of a shock every now and then."

Cliff asked, "Oh, you mean when you meet him at the door in Saran Wrap?"

Becky laughed. No, she said, it was when John met *her* at the door in Saran Wrap! He was the house dad and she was working outside the home.

A little shock, a slight shakeup is a source of energy to get you connected with each other and boost passion.

Way #5: Treat

Treats are endless sources of sexual fun. A woman who can receive loves being treated.

Here are some suggested treats:
- rose petals spread on the sheets when she crawls into bed
- a love nest in front of the fireplace
- an hour of your undivided attention
- an evening to sit and read while you tend the children
- a massage
- time focused completely on what she wants.

Treats that spark a woman's sexual passion don't tend to be the pornographic type promoted in men's magazines. We recommend treating in these categories: purchases, accoutrements, preparation, attention, and activities.

Purchases don't require spending the family inheritance; little gifts can show your forethought. They might be food the two of you enjoy sharing, a card, music that has a positive memory connected with it, clothing she's been wanting or that makes her more attractive to you—or clothing for you that increases your attractiveness to her.

Accoutrements are little extras that send a message of love. Think of staying at a nice hotel and having your bed turned down and a chocolate mint on your pillow when you return to your room at the end of an evening. It makes you feel special. Accoutrements might include candles lit when she comes from the bathroom or a flower at the bedside.

Preparation shows love by readying the atmosphere for the two of you to be together. Examples: lighting a fireplace, heating or cooling the room, adjusting the lighting, setting the music, showering, shaving, putting on cologne, cleaning up your mess in the bedroom, and organizing the evening so the two of you have time to connect.

Attention may be the biggest winner with your wife. Turn off the television and the computer. Your attention to her on her terms could be the treat of the century. Try it!

Activities that one woman considers a treat may leave another cold; keep your wife's tastes in mind. She may like it if you join her in a bubble bath or shower; she may prefer dinner out before lovemaking; she may love dancing together. Maybe she'd like to spend an evening talking and making out on the couch. Just be sure the activities would be treats for both of you.

Way #6: Pleasure

Our good friend Roland asks, "Why do you guys always talk about *pleasuring?*"

It's true—pleasure is central to our message about sex in marriage. It refers to skin-to-skin touch that makes no demand for arousal or orgasm or any response or action. It's just for the sake of touching and being touched.

No demand means exactly that. Your and her responses to the touch can be pleasant, warm, comfortable, enjoyable, arousing, or neutral. The pleasuring can be an end in itself, or it can lead to an erotic lovemaking experience.

The time you take to pleasure and the extent of bodily involvement can vary. Even five minutes will build positive connection. A more extended time can focus on the whole body.

Pleasuring can be done in many ways. Try a foot caress. Or use any part of your body, other than your hands, to touch. Your hair, your nose, your forearms, and even your toes can be used.

Maybe you'd like combing or brushing each other's hair. Cliff doesn't care for that, but he can always count on Joyce relaxing if he strokes her hair.

Cuddling is another form of giving and receiving pleasure. Lying in each other's arms, feeling one another's bodies, may build closeness that leads to more intense passion—or just meshing and relaxation. Cuddling can be with clothes on, in nightclothes, or in the nude.

Way #7: Tease

Teasing can be fun, or it can sting. Each spouse has a unique history when it comes to teasing and being teased. Each of you must be sensitive to the other and take responsibility to let the other know your teasing limits.

In Chapter 3 we recommended teasing touch as a way to keep your wife hungry for more and to let her lead in the sexual experience.

Tickling is another form of teasing that some couples enjoy.

Verbal teasing includes razzing and poking fun at yourself or each other. Take care, however; verbal teases can quickly cross the line from fun to irritation.

Teases that are passive expressions of anger have no place in lovemaking. Keep all teasing fun, light, and free of personal jabs.

Way #8: Resist

Playful resisting can be great fun.

When you sense you've moved in on her a little too eagerly, quickly switch to playing hard to get. You both know she can get you in a second if she wants to, but your playful resistance will be a positive lure.

Try pretending to be asleep, claiming you have a headache, or saying you're not really interested tonight after all. You're just setting her up to come after you, of course. If you tend to push for more too quickly, the silliness of playful resistance can be a good way to break the habit.

Way #9: Create

Creative approaches to sex have a way of sparking interest, heightening arousal, building intensity, and communicating a message of love.

For example, you might create your own special setting for sexual times. One couple turned a mobile home, which had been set up for canning vegetables in summer, into a retreat from the children. Another couple made a love nest in a sewing room. Another man invited his wife to his office, where he had a romantic dinner brought in and served.

You may have a van or pickup camper you can use for romping—or a guest bedroom, a comforter on the floor, or another private spot.

Creativity doesn't require a lot of money or time. The summer after we were married, we worked as interim pastors for a small church in central Canada. Our home had one tiny bed, one table, and two chairs. We carried our water down the street and used the outdoor "biffy."

Yet we found ways to turn our austere situation into fun. We discovered that a creaky wire-spring bed can add pleasure when used correctly! With no money and the promise of not much more to come, we had exciting times together.

Way #10: Play

Playing at sex is the most fun of all.

Play house. Play doctor. Play "I'll show you mine if you'll show me yours."

Play charades. Act out the Song of Solomon. Choose your own forms of play.

Pretending can be a good way to play, as long as you're not deceiving each other. You'll probably spend most of your time laughing while you're pretending.

When you get right down to it, sex can be a hilarious time together. Whether your play is carefully planned or spontaneous, learn to enjoy the wife God has given you by having plenty of fun.

CHAPTER TWELVE

SEX AND YOUR SENSES

You know the five senses—sight, smell, touch, taste, and hearing. We'd add a sixth—your empathetic sense.

All these senses affect the sexual experience for you and your wife. They're gates to sexuality. You can use one gate or many to enter the experience and to connect totally with your spouse.

Are you using all your senses to move toward a more passionate, intimate, and intense sexual life? This chapter can help you do just that.

USE ALL OF YOUR SENSES

1. Seeing

Men are visual responders. You know what kinds of sights trigger you sexually; you know what you need to avoid.

You can use your visual responsiveness to your wife to build your sexual relationship—or shut it down. Let's say you get aroused at the sight of your wife undressing or wearing seductive clothes. If your response to her launches you into immediate action, she'll probably learn to dress cautiously and not change clothes in front of you. Her caution will decrease her sexuality and your pleasure.

On the other hand, if you use your responsiveness to honor her with your praise and enjoyment—without action—she may invite you into her sexual world and find greater enjoyment of her sexuality.

Women don't tend to respond to visual input in the way men do. Yes, it's important for you to look attractive and take care of yourself, but that's just a doorway to her respect that might lead to sexual interest later. The visual is necessary for the relationship, but may not be a direct turn-on.

If you walked into the room to find your wife lying on the bed in a provocative pose and wearing something sexually enticing, you'd probably hope to ravish her body. But if you were to lie on the bed with an erection and wait for her, she'd probably be put off by the demand she would feel. Yet many men have the idea that the aroused man is a draw to the woman. When the woman is interested or aroused, she'll enjoy the man's sexuality; but for most women, the man's arousal isn't a starting point.

Men and women often see an erection as a demand for ejaculation. When that happens, it's a negative visual stimulus for the woman. But the fact is that you started having erections within minutes after you were born and have one every 80 to 90 minutes while you sleep. They're part of the ebb and flow of life. If the two of you recognize that your erection is an involuntary, passing response that doesn't require ejaculation or intercourse, your wife will be more likely to view your erection as user-friendly.

Both of you can learn to use your visual gate to enhance your sexual experiences. Keeping your eyes open before and during lovemaking can build intimacy and intensity. If the two of you are used to having your eyes closed, try keeping them open a little at a time. Seeing can be one more fun ingredient of your sexual times.

2. Smelling

Chemistry between lovers may be based mainly on smell. Perhaps you've read about research on pheromones, the sexual scents animals give off at mating time. The current suspicion is that human beings emit odors that attract selected members of the opposite sex. You and your wife may send off scents that invite or repel each other.

The smells of body lotion, perfume, and aftershave tend to enhance sexual attractiveness, at least in our culture. Since perfumes react differently on the skin of different people, it might be fun to visit a department store together and discover which types you like best on each other.

Natural body odors of arousal, perspiration, and sexual secretions also have the capacity to attract. Their arousal capability varies from culture to culture and time to time. In days past, the musky odors of no bathing were experienced as a sexual invitation for a man; Napoleon wrote to his wife, asking her not to bathe because he was coming home. You would probably write the exact opposite.

Odors are a sensitive, personal matter. Breath, body, hair, genitals, and feet can drive a spouse away. To honor your wife, care for your body and respect her needs for cleanliness and pleasant smells.

If her odors offend you, be gentle in telling her so. A talk away from the bedroom would be wise.

Don't expect your wife to be responsive if you haven't taken care of your body. Generally speaking, she's the best judge of whether or not you have. Her love for you isn't enough to cover bad smells.

3. Touching

Touching is the primary sense used during sex. Every square centimeter of your body has thousands of receptors that take in and transmit the touch to the brain.

A woman may feel loved when receiving a light butterfly touch, a whispery touch, tickles, or a warm, firm touch. A man feels pleasure when he touches certain curves on a woman's body. Her waist, calves, feet, the silkiness of her skin, the contours of her breasts—all provide sensations of enjoyment.

A man's appreciation of his wife's body can be a beautiful experience or a tense one. Conflict erupts when the man assumes a right to the woman's body and won't let her be the authority on how she wants to be touched.

Next time you and your wife are together, let her guide your touch. If she's unwilling or unable to do that, lighten your touch by at least half. Don't increase the firmness until she invites it.

Keep your touch general until she wants it to be more specific. We can almost guarantee that within a week or two, your wife will notice and reinforce your new way of touching.

4. Tasting

The tastes of sex are mostly subtle.

Feeding each other or eating together can add sensuousness to your sexual experience. Most tastes of sex, however, will be experienced as lips and tongue happen to land on each other's bodies and mouths.

The wonderful miracle of kissing will be your most used avenue of sensuous tasting. Kissing is the most personal, intimate part of the sexual experience—perhaps even more personal than getting genitals together. You give yourself to your wife when you passionately kiss her.

Kissing and tasting each other's bodies can be another way to open yourselves to each other. These tastes are one of a kind; they represent your particular relationship and are probably part of what draws you together.

Portions of the Song of Solomon can be taken as a beautiful, symbolic description of a bride and bridegroom tasting each other: "Let my beloved come to his garden and eat its pleasant fruits" (4:16, NKJV). King Solomon says, "I have come to my garden. . . . I have eaten my honeycomb with my honey" (5:1, NKJV).

The lovers of the Song of Solomon may refer to the genitals as the garden of spices. Using the mouth to enjoy a spouse's genitals has been a topic of controversy for generations; be sensitive to your wife's feelings about this practice.

Each of you will be keenly aware of and affected by how the other tastes. Keep yourselves clean for each other, and respect each other's boundaries.

5. Hearing

Your ears can greatly enhance a sexual encounter. During sex, they take in words of love, noises of responsiveness, and even background music or other sounds you've chosen.

Are the words you share in the throes of lovemaking terms of adoration, delight, and appreciation? We hope so. Words of correction or criticism, on the other hand, distract and hurt. What you say during sexual intimacy must be carefully chosen.

The noises of your bodies and your voices communicate the excitement of the moment and the level of intensity you're experiencing. The involuntary expressions can bring even more arousal.

If you're a silent lover, take heed. The gasps, moans, groans, grunts, and deep breathing of sexual response probably would be music to the ears of your lover and bring great joy. If you've never learned to let out your sexual intensity, practice the breathing and sounds of a sexual experience.

Providing background sound can be another sensuous addition. You may like music or a CD of ocean waves or rainfall. Have fun listening to a variety of possibilities to find ones you'd both enjoy during your sexual times. Background sounds can also shield you from others' noises—and others from yours.

6. Empathetic Sensing

Empathy is the ability to connect with the feelings, thoughts, and desires of another person—in this case, the one you've promised to love for her lifetime. According to one dictionary, "Empathy is more enduring and valuable than romantic love."[1]

Why have we added empathy as a sixth sense? Because it's so important to true sexual union.

As you're paying attention to your other senses, you need to respect and respond to your wife's signals and your sense of what's going on in her body. Listen to her and let her pursue pleasure for herself. Connect with her thoughts and feelings as she takes responsibility to know herself and share herself with you.

Empathy isn't guessing what your wife wants or trying to be the authority on her desires. It's paying attention to the signals she shares with you.

Your empathetic sense brings you and your wife together in the powerful, mystical union of "becoming one flesh." Sexual union including empathy is truly becoming one in spirit and mind as well as body.

That fusion makes sex in marriage powerfully erotic, intense, spiritual, and overwhelming. When this union takes place, it transcends our earthbound lives.

USE YOUR MIND, TOO

While you're using your senses, use your mind, too.

The brain manages sexual functioning through the chemicals it secretes, the nervous system it regulates, and the muscles it controls. It also houses all mental images.

The ability to create pictures in your mind is called imagination. It's part of your having been created in God's image. You can think, feel, and project.

> **KEY CONCEPT:**
> The capacity for fantasizing is God-given; the responsibility for the content of the fantasy is personal.

Images, including sexual ones, can drift across your mind even when you haven't chosen them. These passing pictures will be influenced by what you put into your mind—what you see on television or in the movies, what you read in books or hear in songs, or what you've experienced. You can even find yourself thinking about images that seem to have no source in your recent or even distant past.

You're responsible for what you choose to put into your mind, and for what you do with images that involuntarily enter there. You can choose to nurture and build positive images, and you can reject negative ones.

As the apostle Paul wrote,

> Finally, brethren, whatever is true, whatever is honorable, whatever is right, whatever is pure, whatever is lovely, whatever is of good repute, if there is any excellence and if anything worthy of praise, let your mind dwell on these things (Philippians 4:8).

Your responsibility is to put pictures into your mind that honor your marriage and your relationship with God.

The capacity for fantasizing is God-given; the responsibility for the content of the fantasy is personal.

God designed you to be sexually responsive. That responsiveness is not selective. But God calls you to be selective in what you pursue in your mind and in your actions.

Sexual intimacy and fulfillment were designed for marriage. Anything that distorts that union or distracts from it turns fantasy to lust and lust to adultery (see Matthew 5:28). For this reason, put the face of your wife in place of any inappropriate picture that enters your mind. Always turn your mind toward home!

Fantasy can build your marital relationship when you and your wife use it to create dreams of mutual enjoyment and pleasure. For instance, you don't have to own a home on the beach to have a romantic interlude there. You can generate that setting in your mind.

Joseph Dillow, in *Solomon on Sex*, says, "I think it's time we Christian brothers used some sanctified imagination around our home."[2] Use your mind—and your senses—to be creative, expressive, poetic, enticing, seductive, and intimate with your wife.

CHAPTER THIRTEEN

PORNOGRAPHY AND THE INTERNET

Want a truly great sex life?
Want to fulfill your biblical calling to honor your wife?
Want to raise your kids in a godly way?
Then stay away from pornography!

WHAT'S SO BAD ABOUT ONE LITTLE WEB SITE?

The primary pipeline for bringing pornography home these days is the Internet. This powerfully addictive force is invading marriages and families like yours, with a destructive impact beyond most people's imaginations.

The Rise of Internet Porn

Twenty-five years ago, getting a pornographic "fix" was hard work. A man had to go to a sleazy part of town, park his car some distance away, pull his hat down over his eyes and lift up his collar, look about furtively, and slink into an adult bookstore or massage parlor.

The need to sneak started changing when pornographic videos

became available for rent. Still, the process of getting them held the danger of embarrassment or discovery.

The risk was reduced with cable television, which brought porn right into the home. But there were still limits. A subscription was required, and could be discovered by others. A visitor surfing the channels might notice. And the TV was usually centrally located, making it hard to watch without detection.

Then came the Internet—introducing the greatest possibilities for variety and privacy.

Last time we checked, there were 137,000,000 (yes, that's million) Web sites under the subject of sex. Surely some of those are healthy sites that offer medical and psychological information, including our own *www.passionatecommitment.com*. The great majority, however, are pornographic.

If you started visiting these sites at a rate of a hundred per day, it would take thousands of years to visit them all—not to mention those that would be added each day. At this writing, sites are being added at the rate of one million per month.

By the time you read this, who knows how many sites there will be? The only sure thing is that there will continue to be an endless supply of sexual material, most of it garbage and most of it addicting.

Ease of access to Internet porn is staggering. It's available on the computer in your home or office; you can view it in complete privacy. Sites don't screen for your age, they're available twenty-four hours a day, and thousands of them are free. You can visit for five minutes, five hours, or five days at a time. There's always new material, featuring every possible sexual variation or deviation.

And no one gets hurt, right?

Wrong!

Effects on Your Marriage

Some guys think occasional viewing of pornography is harmless. But it can hurt your relationship with your wife as well as your relationship with God.

Even casual viewing of pornography can change how a man thinks and feels about women, and how he treats them. This has been called the "centerfold syndrome." Looking at idealized images of shapely women offering themselves in the most provocative ways changes how you see your wife. She'll seem less attractive, unable to compete with these pictures.

> Even casual viewing of pornography can change how a man thinks and feels about women, and how he treats them.

It's wrong to force your wife to compete with fantasy women. It may very well make her seem inadequate.

Pornography also degrades women, making them mere objects designed to fulfill men's fantasies. It precludes any possibility of intimacy. How can anyone be intimate with a series of pixels on a computer screen?

Men and women were created to share the deepest parts of themselves, not to be mechanisms for another's sexual gratification. When you enter the world of pornography, you opt out of intimacy. Your relationship with your wife—to all women—goes off track.

Effects on Your Children

What happens if children discover their father is visiting pornographic sites?

A boy who looks up to his dad probably would get the message that pornography is okay. A daughter could be confused at best; during adolescence, when a girl begins to find she's a sexual being, she needs to see her father cherishing her mother. Discovering that he looks at perverse images of female sexuality could make her cynical about men, or cause her to feel dirty or uncertain about her own sexuality.

Some men may think they can keep their Web surfing a secret from family members. But most Internet browsers include a "history" function, which lists sites you've visited recently. Many spouses and probably most adolescents are aware of this feature, and may check to see where you've been. Yes, you can erase your history. But that in itself could raise suspicions.

Do You Have a Problem?

Most sexual addictions begin early in life, usually between the ages of eight and fifteen. Not so with the Internet. We find that many people who've never struggled with sexual addiction get hooked on Internet porn in their thirties, forties, and fifties. Men—and some women—of every educational and socioeconomic level are potential addicts.

If you struggle with any of the following, you have a problem. Do you . . .

- Visit sexual sites on the Web?
- Go to sexually oriented chat rooms?
- Keep these visits a secret from family, friends, and co-workers?
- Masturbate in response to Internet content?
- Find that your viewing affects your marital relationship, sexual life, work production, sleep patterns, feelings about yourself, or relationship with God?

- Design your life around Web surfing?
- Lie more and more to cover your Internet activities?
- Need ever more titillating material to get you aroused?
- Download material from sexual sites?
- Put sites on your "favorites" list for easy access?
- Pay for certain sites and hide these charges?
- Clear out your "history" regularly?
- Lose track of time while searching for the "perfect" image?
- Take risks by meeting in person with chat-room connections?

Chances are that you know deep down whether the Internet is a problem for you. That struggle won't go away by itself. It will not evaporate because of willpower, or feeling terrible afterward, or confessing it, or promising God you'll never do it again, or white-knuckling it for a few days or a week. You need help!

What Is a Sexual Addiction?

An Internet porn addiction is one kind of sexual addiction. Simply stated, if you lack control of a sexual behavior, you're struggling with a sexual addiction.

The sexual addict feels controlled by the urge in the same way an overeater is controlled by the eating disorder or an alcoholic is controlled by the urge to drink. If he's married, his preoccupation interferes with his marriage; he isn't satisfied by an intimate sexual relationship with his spouse.

> A sexual addict isn't satisfied by an intimate sexual relationship with his spouse.

When the sexual urge is pressing, the addict feels anxious; he's captured by the drive. Afterward he's guilty, ashamed. This secret drive escalates to become the major focus of his life. It's his way of hiding from realities he doesn't want to face.

Sexual addiction provides an adrenaline high that perpetuates the behavior. It's similar to relying on cocaine or marijuana. The addict feels he's no longer able to make choices about his activities, but is compelled to engage in them even though he'll hate himself later.

Not every wrong sexual behavior is an addiction. For example, some men occasionally view pornographic material or go to a topless bar, but are not hooked on those activities. We're not implying that these are advisable or morally acceptable—they're not! But sexual addictions have obsessive and compulsive qualities that drive the person almost against his own will to act them out.

Sexual addiction may be a symptom of underlying, unmet emotional and relational needs. The person may have an addictive personality that tends to "zone out" or "split off" from his real self and act in ways that differ from his usual personality and convictions.

Dr. Patrick Carnes has been a pioneer in the study and treatment of sexual addiction. He first brought the subject to public awareness with his best-selling book *Out of the Shadows: Understanding Sexual Addiction* (Hazelden Information Education, 2001). He has also written *Sexual Anorexia: Overcoming Sexual Self-Hatred* (Hazelden Information Education, 1997) and *In the Shadow of the Net: Breaking Free of Compulsive Online Sexual Behavior* (Hazelden Information Education, 2001).

We've come to believe in Carnes' formulations because they fit so well with our clinical experience. We've also come to accept his treatment approach because it's the only one we've found to work.

We're indebted to Carnes for virtually every concept presented here.

The Addictive Pattern

As the sexually addicted person retreats from normal relationships with wife, family, co-workers, and friends, he moves into his own world. In that world he carries on a secret life. The loneliness grows, propelling him ever further into his private realm.

The addict's aloneness reinforces his belief about himself—that he's an undesirable person no one can love. He becomes more convinced that only he can meet his deep needs. Sex seems to be the deepest need and promises to fill the void.

Because relationships have usually brought pain, the addict avoids closeness. In fact, sexual addiction and avoiding intimacy almost always go together. Neither the Internet nor magazines demand a relationship; the images cooperate completely. The addict never has to give of himself.

This self-centeredness is rationalized:

"I deserve it."

"I work hard."

"My sexual needs aren't being met."

"It doesn't hurt anyone."

If you use these "explanations" to excuse your sexual behavior, you're struggling with an addiction whether you know it or not.

WHAT TO DO IF YOU HAVE A PROBLEM

If you find your preoccupation with sex on the Internet (or any other sexual habit) growing, and you're acting on that impulse with ever greater frequency, you have reason for concern. Maybe you've tried to control your habit, but always find yourself back and more involved than before.

Here are five steps you can take.

Step 1: Start with the Heart

If you're hooked, acknowledge that the addiction won't go away by itself. Only God's power and the help of His people will enable you to break the chains of addiction. Until you admit that you're powerless and decide to turn your life, will, and actions over to God, nothing will change.

Remember the parable of the prodigal son? When he'd tried everything, he found himself in the pigpen. The King James version says it so clearly in Luke 15:17-18: "And when he came to himself, he said. . . . I will arise and go to my father . . ."

The starting point of change is the moment of repentance when you "come to yourself." You face yourself in the mirror, accept the reality of your powerlessness, hit bottom, and put your life in God's hands.

If you've been "busted" by your wife, husband, boss, or kids and are only acknowledging what they know, you haven't truly repented. It's time for a full moral inventory and admission of your sin before God and to those you've wronged. The first step is a change of heart.

Step 2: Change Your Life Patterns

To stop drinking, an alcoholic has to "get the booze out of the kitchen." That by itself won't control the addiction, but it's a necessary step. Going to a bar to hang around with old drinking buddies has to stop.

What needs to be changed for you? It depends on your addiction. If you always buy pornography at a certain shop, you can never go there again. If the massage parlor or strip joint is on your normal route home, choose a different route.

If you "act out" during business travel, you can stay only in hotels that have no "adult" movies. If that's not possible, have the front desk shut off access to those movies—just as an alcoholic would refuse to take the minibar key.

If the Internet is your area of struggle, take these steps:

- At home and in the office, always have the computer screen facing the door—so that anyone who walks by or into the room can see it.
- Put the computer in a central, high-traffic room in your home.
- Get a filter that blocks pornography sites.
- Give all passwords to your wife.
- Teach your spouse to check the history on your Web browser at random times.
- Never use the computer when you're the only one at home or the only one awake.
- Go to bed at the same time as your spouse.
- Identify and avoid the pattern associated with logging onto sexual sites; for instance, if you tend to do it when your wife goes to a weekly meeting, spend that time in the presence of others.
- Stop masturbating in response to Internet content.
- Select someone to whom you'll be accountable at home, at work, or wherever you struggle; set a check-in time with that person.
- Seriously consider ending your Internet access and getting an e-mail-only system.

Step 3: Focus on the Internal You

When repentance has taken place and you've changed direction, the long haul begins.

This is a war. You have to attack from the air, the sea, the ground, and outer space.

What does that mean in real life?

Join others to "work the steps." An accountability group can walk you through a 12-step process. Commit yourself to that process.

Don't concern yourself with group labels. What's necessary is regularly facing your powerlessness, your dependence on God, and your flawed moral character. Be willing to make amends—and, perhaps for the first time, live an honest and open life. Such involvement in a group is central; we rarely see long-term change without it!

Learn new ways to think about your sexuality. Read books by Dr. Patrick Carnes, especially *Out of the Shadows* and *In The Shadows of the Net.* Read *Faithful and True* (Zondervan, 1996) by Mark Laaser, a good friend who struggled his way out of a sexual addiction; he has been on Carnes' team of professionals and has a biblical and psychological perspective. His three-part video series (*The Geneva Series* from the American Association of Christian Counselors, Nashville, Tennessee) is practical and offers a powerful message of hope for marital restoration.

There are other resources—books, tapes, videos, and programs—that can be of great help, too. Don't try to go it alone; that rarely works.

To bring healing to your emotions, you may need to get into therapy. A caring, insightful, biblically guided counselor can help you work through wounds from the past and the low self-concept that led in part to your addiction. You'll be served best by a therapist who understands and regularly works with sexual addictions.

Step 4: Focus on Your Relationships

Your relationships also need changing, especially those with God and your spouse.

Sexual misbehavior has strained your relationship with God. You've probably cycled through many rounds of acting out, despair, anguished confessions, sincere promises, and earnest devotion—only to find yourself practicing your addictive behavior again.

You may have rationalized your behavior, denying it had any detrimental effect. But all the while you knew you were rebelling against God, and violating yourself and your marriage.

> Be willing to make amends—and, perhaps for the first time, live an honest and open life.

Get into a group or class where you can connect with others as you grow spiritually. Recommit yourself to practice the disciplines of Bible study, prayer, worship, and service. The work of God's Spirit in your life is essential to your healing.

It's important to work on developing your capacity for intimacy with your spouse. This includes not just sexual intimacy, but first and foremost emotional and spiritual intimacy. Since you may have spent a lifetime avoiding intimacy, this may be the hardest dimension of the healing process.

At first it will have to be intentional—talking, reading, praying, connecting. It won't come naturally.

After focusing on emotional and spiritual intimacy with your spouse, begin building sexual intimacy. This will help fill the void you were trying to satisfy with your addictive behavior.

When a husband comes to us ready to let go of his sexual addiction, we bring his wife into the therapy soon after control is established. We take the couple through a sexual retraining process from our book *Restoring the Pleasure,* concentrating on touching, talking, and teaching exercises to build sexual intimacy. You may want a counselor to help you do the same.

Step 5: Be Accountable

Remember, you can't do this alone! You need to be accountable to someone.

In 12-step programs, this person is called a sponsor. The title doesn't matter. What matters is that you have someone with whom you're totally and bluntly honest.

There can be no secrets with this person. If you're going to heal, you need complete openness. That means you fully trust this person's confidentiality and judgment. You're also confident that your good is his highest concern.

Hope for Healing

So how do you get control of an Internet pornography addiction—or any other sexual addiction?

- You face yourself and your powerlessness.
- You have a change of heart as you throw yourself at God's feet, repentant and ready for His healing.
- You set up external controls that help you change your behavior.
- You pursue internal changes that lead you to be the authentic person God created you to be.

Even casual use of Internet pornography will damage your relationship with your wife and keep you from having the great sex life you both desire. Make a covenant with your family that you won't visit those sites.

If you can't keep that promise, take it as an indication that you need help—and get it.

CHAPTER FOURTEEN

A WORD TO THE WIVES IS SUFFICIENT

If you're a wife who's sneaking a look at this book, we'll assume that you've read the previous chapters. Actually, we encourage that. But they're really for your husband.

If you're a husband, you need to know that this chapter is for your wife. We'd encourage you to read it, too.

But we have some ground rules for both of you. Neither of you is to comment or complain about the other doing his or her part. Each of you is responsible for your attitude and approach to making your sexual life more fulfilling.

From this point on, we'll address the wife as "you." Guys, feel free to follow along.

ENJOY THE PROCESS

Just as men like results, women like the process. When a woman joins a man in a goal-oriented approach to sex, sex may be great initially, but the spark dies quickly.

Your mother and your friends may have told you that sex is

primarily for the man. They were wrong! If you don't think of sex as being for you, you have goals similar to his.

You may believe other myths, too:

- that you should be interested anytime he is
- that you should get aroused when he goes straight for your sexual buttons
- that you need to focus on pleasuring him and give up the possibility of your own enjoyment
- that you must have an orgasm or half a dozen orgasms.

> Goal-oriented sex won't work any better for you than it does for him.

You may have lost interest in sex because you've felt like a failure. You haven't achieved the goals you thought were important to satisfy him and have a happy sex life.

Whatever the demands you've placed on yourself or him, goal-oriented sex won't work any better for you than it does for him.

Sex is about the process of enjoying mutual pleasure, not about your pleasing him or his pleasing you. Ultimately, your husband will be pleased when you're pleased, and you'll be pleased when you respond to your natural instincts of extending and enjoying pleasure.

Focus on pleasure rather than on stimulation. Let stimulation be the by-product if it happens. If it doesn't, you've had a good time and made a warm connection; that's the most important part.

If a musician strains to hit a high or low note, it won't work because she's trying too hard. If she lets it flow from deep inside her, she'll be able to open up and let the beautiful notes resonate. The same is true in sex. As you're able to let go and focus on the pleasure of the sexual experience, you'll find the greatest excitement, arousal, and ecstasy.

LISTEN TO YOUR BODY

Good sex doesn't just happen, but you can make it happen by listening to your body. You're the authority on what your body needs and wants.

> **You can make good sex happen by listening to your body; you're the authority on what your body needs and wants.**

Society isn't your authority. Neither are magazines—or even books. Medical doctors can help, but they can't know what your body is telling you. Neither can your husband.

You can discover with your husband what you enjoy and communicate that to him. Don't expect him to know how long or how hard or where or in what order you like to be touched. Take responsibility to know and tell how you would like to make love.

How do you learn to listen to your body? You begin to pay attention to the messages it gives. You respect the signals and take them seriously.

You may notice your desire as an urge for closeness and touch. You might feel edgy as an indication of your need for release. Or you may experience genital sensations.

Listen to your body during the sexual experience, too. How do you like to start? Do you prefer deep, passionate kissing, or is that better for you once you get aroused? Do you prefer to begin with pleasuring him, being pleasured, or enjoying each other's bodies simultaneously? What about breast stimulation? If you don't like your nipples turned like dials on a radio, you're pretty normal. Invite the touch you like.

You may have to teach your husband genital touching and guide him, to some extent, in every experience. You may or may not want entry, thrusting, or an orgasm. In any case, let him know.

Communicate how you like to complete your sexual times, too. If you've had intercourse, you may prefer to stay united and hold each other and caress and talk. Or you may wish to separate, get cleaned up, and fall asleep. Express what you desire, respect what he desires, and negotiate a combination that satisfies both.

A Caution

Paying attention to your body's signals isn't the same as spectatoring. As we said in Chapter 5, monitoring how you're doing will get in the way of your body's experience. Sex works best when you get lost in enjoying each other and satisfying the hunger inside you—not when you keep close track of your body or your husband's responses.

One woman asked us what was getting in the way of her sexual arousal and release. We asked her to picture exactly what she and her husband did and what she felt in response.

> **Sex works best when you get lost in enjoying each other and satisfy the hunger inside you.**

She led us through their last sexual event, evaluating her body's response instead of describing feelings. For example, she said, "When he stroked me all over my body, I got lubricated. But his touching my clitoris did nothing. Then when I asked him to go inside my vagina, I got aroused, so I told him and everything stopped." She'd halted her body's automatic responses by spectatoring.

Another woman reported her husband's level of enthusiasm or boredom. She watched whether he had his eyes open or closed, whether he seemed excited enough, and whether he was pleased with her level of response. She lessened her response by indirectly evaluating herself through him.

> To counteract watching, become an active player because you can't watch and play at the same time.

Watching creates self-consciousness and interrupts pleasure. To counteract it, become an active player. You can't watch and play at the same time.

LEARN TO LEAD

Learn to lead with your sexuality, not with demand or control.

The thought of leading may be scary to you, especially if you believe your husband should be the sexual expert and know how to please you. He may have no more of a clue on how to follow than you do on how to lead. What a wonderful opportunity for the two of you to learn and discover together!

Here are five keys to learning how to lead.

Key #1: Know Your Body
To know your sexual self, you may need to do a genital self-exam, read a book, watch a video, or attend a seminar. Much of the discovery can happen between your husband and you.

Find out how you fit the generalizations we've made in this

book about women—and how you're different. Your uniqueness must be clarified.

Discover how your hormonal pattern influences your mood and your sexual interest. You may want to keep a monthly diary to help. Are you most sexually interested at ovulation, for example? Before or right after your period? Is it different if you're on the pill?

> As you lovingly communicate and take responsibility for your conditions, you invite his respect and bring the two of you closer.

Key #2: Know Your Conditions
Women tend to have more conditions for sex than men do. Knowing and communicating yours will make sex better for both of you.

Whether your conditions are little or big, they need to be respected. For example, you may have discovered that the best way for you to get into the experience is to first have a time of talking or holding and hugging and kissing. This wouldn't be uncommon. If connecting time leads you most naturally into the sexual experience, listen to that need and take responsibility to make sure it happens.

If being grabbed shuts you down sexually, don't let it happen. Guide him to an alternative.

Perhaps you need him to shave before sex—or get up and lock the bedroom door. Or you may need serious attention to needs that come from past sexual abuse or having been raised in an alcoholic home.

If you lovingly communicate your conditions while taking responsibility for them, he'll be more likely to respect them—and the two of you will move closer together.

Key #3: Know Your Sexual Triggers

Sexual triggers are actions or environments that switch on your sexual energy. Certain music, body pampering, or even vacationing in a hot, dry climate are sure triggers for some women.

You probably know what "winds your clock." Maybe it's your husband's words of praise, conversation, a call of care from the office, help around the house, a love note, flowers, touch without sexual expectation, tender kisses, affirmation of your sexuality, or his undressing you. Share this awareness with him.

What triggers your sexual energy today might not be the same tomorrow. Be confident enough to keep explaining what puts you in the mood.

Key #4: Know Your Husband

One woman said, "Since the primary sex organ is supposed to be the brain, my husband should never have any problems with sex because that is all that is on his mind."

Some men experience love through sex. They pursue sex far more frequently than is necessary to meet their physical needs. They may work on averages, figuring that if they get sex once for every eight times they ask, they'll keep asking to get that one out of eight.

If this describes your husband, he may be insecure about getting love if he lets you initiate. You may need to make a deal: If a week goes by and nothing has happened, he's free to start the process.

On the other hand, your husband may be quite the opposite. He may be intimidated by sex or by intimacy, and may experience your sexual needs as pressure. Lead in ways that don't resemble demands. For example, being physically close and stroking his genitals may be easier to take than a verbal message of your need—or vice versa.

If spontaneity is difficult for him, scheduling or giving advance notice may work better than expecting him to respond at the drop of a hat. If scheduling makes him feel controlled, try planning ahead but don't forewarn him.

Your husband also may be anxious about his sexual adequacy. Affirm his positive efforts; when he moves in your direction, reinforce him.

Key #5: Learn to Take

Is it hard for you to receive sexual pleasure? If so, maybe you've accepted one or more of these myths:

- sexual pleasure is not for women
- a woman's sexual duty is to keep her man satisfied so he won't roam away from home
- if he's happy, you're happy
- nice women aren't overtly sexual.

Or you may have stopped expressing your sexuality because of past trauma, living with a sexually demanding husband, or feeling you have no value except as the receptacle of his sexual aggression.

To lead sexually in your marriage, you must learn to take. You have to give yourself permission to take in compliments, pleasure, and stimulation.

Sex is for you as well as for your husband. That's the way your body is designed. God created you with a clitoris that has no other purpose than to receive and transmit sexual stimulation. Even the vagina is designed for both pleasure and procreation.

Before you can lead, you need to be able to enjoy three things:
• your own sexuality
• your husband's delight in your sexuality, and
• your pleasure in his sexuality.
You don't have to put aside your needs in order to please your husband. In fact, you'll please him more by going after pleasure for yourself and taking in his enjoyment of you.

LEAD HIM TO INTIMACY

Growing up, girls develop the capacity for intimacy in ways that often aren't as available or as natural for boys. Girls tend to share more time with their mothers than boys do with their fathers. Girls work out their emotions by talking with each other; boys tend to process their feelings in seclusion.

Chances are that you need to take the lead in nurturing intimacy. Your felt need for and comfort with intimacy may be greater than his, even though he'll enjoy it when it happens.

Accept His Need for Space
When you pursue intimacy with your husband, he'll probably get close, then need "space," then be ready to move close again. Think in electrical terms: A man works best with an alternating current of closeness and intimacy. He tends to short out with a direct current of ongoing intimacy. The amount of time he feels the need for intimacy varies from man to man and from day to day.

What do we mean by alternating? Talking in fifteen-minute or half-hour blocks with plenty of space in between will be much more manageable for a lot of men than an hour-and-a-half or two-hour discussion. Sharing for an extended period of time every few days will be a lot easier than daily in-depth conversations.

Balance Your Needs and His

Many activities can distract a man from his need for intimacy. A game that's important to him, a fishing trip, or a day of golf can become a priority over closeness with you. You may feel replaced. Don't think of it as a message about you; he'd be the same with whomever he was married to.

As you accept his needs and still express yours, the two of you can find ways to get both met. Time your "close encounters" so that they take both spouses' needs into consideration.

And don't announce your intimacy times with a statement like, "Let's share," "Let's communicate," or "Let's be intimate." That creates self-consciousness. Try working them into your daily life together or at scheduled talk times.

Sex and Romance

You may have romantic images of how marriage and sex should be. Perhaps you haven't shared these dreams with your husband, but you're frustrated that he hasn't fulfilled them. Take responsibility to communicate these expectations.

You may ask, "But how can romance be romantic if I do that?" If you realize your vision of romance, it will be romantic. If you expect him to intuitively know what you consider romantic, you'll be disappointed—and he'll lose confidence in trying.

Or you may say, "If he loved me, he would do the romantic part." His romantic attentiveness, or lack of it, probably has nothing to do with how much he loves you. The way his brain works and his comfort with romantic efforts shape what he does or doesn't do.

If you absolutely require him to create the romance for you, talk about your need with him. Let him know some small expressions of romance you'd like. When he attempts to take action, reinforce his efforts. With time, he may even create some romance on his own.

Blocks to Intimacy

The anger, shame, abuse, abandonment, and low self-esteem mentioned in Chapter 6 could be your issues as well. If you've brought such destructive patterns into your marriage, you may do well to seek professional help to sort them out.

Sex may become the battleground for working out other marital issues. One woman didn't want to pursue sexuality for herself because she knew it would make her husband happy. She preferred not to have pleasure if it might be positive for him.

When wives and husbands come to us for sexual therapy, we're often surprised to discover that their desires for their sexual lives are almost identical—even though they think they're miles apart. Other issues have distorted their perceptions.

You may need professional help as you work together to sort out the problems interfering with the intimacy you both want. As you overcome those obstacles, intimacy will develop.

WHEN IT ISN'T WORKING

What if your sex life isn't working as it's supposed to? Here are some frequently asked questions.

What If He Wants It and I Don't?

How often should you feel desire? There's no formula. But if you never sense an urge in your body for sexual contact, pleasure, arousal, or release, you need to attend to that absence.

Life events, bodily functioning, or relationship issues may have gotten in the way of your sexual desire. It may be a result of how you were raised, some violating experience you suffered, hormonal imbalance, or a troubled relationship. Whatever it is, you can deal with it—but only you can get the help you need from a doctor or counselor.

What If "Going for It" Is Giving in to Him?

One woman said, "I wouldn't initiate sex whenever I wanted it. I would be afraid that if I had it whenever I wanted it, he would get used to having it too often."

Perhaps you won't "go for it" because you're afraid it would shackle you with demands. Or the bondage of anger toward your husband keeps you from discovering love, passion, and intimacy. That bondage is probably much older than your relationship with him; it may have started with forced early sexuality in your home.

One woman was forced to watch her father urinate when she was a preschooler to teach her about male genitals. Another woman's mother pinched the girl's budding breasts regularly to check their development and determine bra size. Both had their sexuality taken away from them as children or adolescents. Now they have difficulty going for sex for themselves.

Anger can also be traced to losing a father—whether through death, desertion, or emotional distance. You may subconsciously fear that if you freely pursued sex with your husband, he would leave you as your father did.

Even though you may bring the primary issues that cause this struggle, it will seem that he's the cause of your difficulty. He'll have to back off before you can learn to enjoy sex. You'll probably need a counselor's help in this process.

What If My Mind Wanders?

Your mind will wander during sex. Your husband's may also, but not as frequently; when he's aroused, his mind is usually connected with his body's responses.

Since you function on two tracks, you can enjoy physical pleasure even as a mundane thought enters your mind. You may think about the grocery list, the wallpaper you need, or what you're going to pack in the kids' lunches tomorrow. Don't worry about your passing thoughts, as long as they don't sidetrack you from pleasure or take you away from the experience.

If these thoughts become a problem, counteract them by getting active. Talk, change position, listen to your body's hungers and go after them. Shift from passive mode, where your mind isn't engaged.

What If He Has the Headache?

When a man's diminished sexual desire becomes the pattern rather than the exception, the two of you need to discover and deal with the cause.

Lack of sexual desire in a man may be for reasons similar to those of a woman—past abuse or failure, trouble in the marital relationship, struggle with internal turmoil about being sexual, hormone imbalance, or not perceiving himself as a successful lover. Preoccupation with homosexuality, pornography, or other sexual addictions could also cause a man not to be interested in making love with his wife.

Support and participate with your husband in determining and overcoming his lack of desire. Enlist the help of a doctor, counselor, or sexual therapist.

What If He Keeps Forgetting What I've Told Him?

Men may forget during sex for the same reason that their minds aren't likely to wander: Their minds and bodies are totally connected to their arousal and release.

Whatever the cause of his forgetting, it's probably not a sign of his lack of love for you. If he forgets that it hurts when he squeezes your nipples, or when he latches onto one spot and rubs it until it feels like it's going to ignite, gently guide him to an area or activity that's pleasurable for you. Try to do this before the irritating action drives a wedge between you.

> Talking about sex is vital to keeping love, passion, and intimacy alive in your sex life.

Assuming responsibility for yourself doesn't let him off the hook. The previous chapters in this book will help him with his role. But he can't play it without your active involvement.

What If We Have Sex the Same Way Every Time?

Change is difficult, even if you want it. Change takes work. It also takes risk.

Talk to each other and make a plan. One of you may need to assume leadership in bringing more creativity into your sex life.

Which of you is most likely to initiate novelty? You may be married to a man who does exactly the same thing every day when he gets home from work, likes to eat the same meals at the same time, goes to the same restaurants, and does the same chores every Saturday. Why would he be any different in the lovemaking department?

If change is important for you, you'll probably have to see to it that change happens. If you're the stick-in-the-mud, he may have to be more innovative. If neither of you can muster up enough originality to make the changes your sexual relationship needs, consult a book like our *52 Ways to Have Fun, Fantastic Sex* (Thomas Nelson, 1993).

What If All We Ever Have Is Quickies?

What can you do if your sexual experiences are six or seven minutes long and happen late at night or even in the middle of the night?

Talk about your pattern and what each of you would like to do about it. If having longer, quality sexual times is a mutual goal, set aside times when you focus just on pleasuring and caressing each other. If your husband is reluctant to take that time, start by looking for opportunities to pleasure him. Keep your attempts playful, so that neither of you feels pressured.

What If My Sexual Past Has Invaded Our Bedroom?

If your past is your struggle, get help. You may see an individual therapist or join a group of women who've had similar experiences.

Sharing the pain will help you get past the pain. Some women fear this sharing will drive their husbands away; instead, we find most husbands are extremely open and ready to be involved. They want to help their wives deal with the pain and become able to enjoy the sexual experience.

If certain sexual activities are reminders of the abuse, avoid them. For example, if making love in the dark recalls the abuse, make love in the daytime or with the lights on. If a certain touch or noise sets off a panicky reaction in you, plan ways to signal him so that he can adjust. Sometimes major shifts are necessary. If you were abused when you were on your back, for example, you may be able to let go to orgasm only if you are on top.

You can't just forget your painful past. You and your husband can find a path to healing if you deal with it together and out loud.

What If We Don't Talk About Sex?

Choose the setting in which talking is most comfortable. If most of your more intimate relationship conversations have happened away from home, use a time away. Maybe you'd rather walk and talk or drive and talk than sit and look at each other. If you've had your best talks early in the morning or late at night, choose the time most likely to work.

Decide on a way of communicating that will be most effective. Maybe you'd like to read letters from each other and discuss them. Or talk into a tape recorder and listen and react to each other. Or read part of this book aloud to each other and talk about it.

Women tend not to talk about sex after sex. Since sexual performance is important for men and is equated with having a happy wife, an expression of your enjoyment after a time together could be a way to enhance your sexual life.

Talking about your sex life is an absolute must for a healthy sexual relationship. Willingness to share your feelings about this vulnerable area of your marriage affirms your bond and expresses a form of intimacy.

What If I Can't Be Sexual?

Maybe you think none of these words to wives will work for you. You've been trying all your married life and you're convinced you just aren't sexual.

Does it seem God left out the sexual love when He created your brain? Your body may respond, but you don't feel anything; you aren't emotionally connected to the arousal. Or perhaps you try but nothing happens to your body.

"I can't tell him when I'm turned on," one woman said. "I wouldn't want to initiate sex because that would be a sign of my neediness." This woman's mother had many sexual partners after Dad left them when she was two years old. Being sexually out of control was her mother's way of showing neediness. Now the daughter struggles in her sexual relationship with her husband.

Another woman said, "I can enjoy pleasing him, but I don't think I can receive."

There could also be a hormonal reason for your inability to be sexual. Ask your physician to test your hormone levels, particularly your free testosterone level.

Other possible causes include fear of your sexuality and demands you or your husband have placed on you to be sexual. Once you recognize the reason, you still will need to *decide* to be sexual.

Accept that by God's design you are sexual. Start behaving sexually; the actions will precede the feelings. Give yourself at least a year of consistently pursuing sex for yourself with your husband before you get discouraged.

When you think negative thoughts like, "This will never work," verbalize them and distract yourself from them. Tell your husband when such thoughts interrupt your pleasure. Recommit yourself to pursue sexuality by decision, not desire.

Allow him to enjoy your body, whether yours responds or not. Enjoy his body, even if you don't get aroused by it.

What If He Doesn't Turn Me On?
He *can't* turn you on. Only *you* can allow your body to get turned on.

Unless hormones or other physical factors are the issue, allowing your response is your decision. To let yourself be aroused by him, you need to be ready to totally give yourself to him.

You may want to get turned on, but don't want to give yourself to him. You can't have both; it's your choice.

You may need to deal with conflict or anger in your relationship, or issues from your past. You may need to take an inventory of what's changed since the days when you did allow yourself to respond to him—assuming you did. Perhaps sex has always been disappointing, or you're bored with your sex life.

It may take a counselor to discover why you've shut down sexually. He or she can help you know and pursue the issues that keep you from allowing yourself to respond.

What If I'm Not in Love with Him?
Love is a decision, a commitment (see 1 Corinthians 13). Your *feelings* of love can change from day to day.

Love can be hurt. You may decide to no longer love because of hurts—but that's your decision, not something that happens to you. To love him or not is in your control.

We've discovered that when the barrier between spouses can be broken down, their decision of love can be rekindled—and the feeling of "in loveness" can return. Still, the feelings come and go.

That's why feelings can't be the criterion for true love. Feelings enhance the decision to love, and they should be taken seriously. But don't think that the relationship is over because you feel you're no longer in love with him.

TAKE HIS ADVICE

If you've read the previous chapters addressed to your husband, you've already heard much of the rest of the advice we'd give you. Here's a quick summary:

1. Protect your marriage by paying attention to your vulnerability and turning your heart toward home.

2. Plan that erotic adventure with your husband.

3. Use your imagination creatively and wholesomely.

4. Have fun with your sexuality; enjoy yourselves together.

Give yourself permission to be the vibrantly sexual person God designed you to be. Decide to discover and share your sexuality with your husband—and you'll find true love, passion, and intimacy in your marriage.

An excellent wife, who can find? For her worth is far above jewels. The heart of her husband trusts in her, and he will have no lack of gain. She does him good and not evil all the days of her life (Proverbs 31:10-12).

— NOTES —

Chapter 1

1. Leo Buscaglia, *Loving Each Other: The Challenge of Human Relationships* (New York: Holt, Rinehart & Winston, 1984), p. 134.

Chapter 2

1. Lewis B. Smedes, *Love Within Limits: Realizing Selfless Love in a Selfish World* (Grand Rapids, Mich.: Eerdmans, 1978), p. 133.
2. John Trent, et al, *Go the Distance: The Making of a Promise Keeper* (Colorado Springs, Colo.: Focus on the Family, 1996), p. 128.
3. John Gray, *Men Are from Mars, Women Are from Venus* (New York: HarperCollins, 1992), p. 11.
4. Paula M. Siegel, "Can You Psyche Yourself into Sex?" *Self,* December 1990, p. 144.

Chapter 3

1. Archibald Hart, *The Sexual Man* (Dallas: Word Publishing, 1994).
2. John Gray, *Mars and Venus in the Bedroom: A Guide to Lasting Romance and Passion* (New York: HarperCollins, 1995), p. 35.

Chapter 4

1. *Los Angeles Times,* February 5, 1996.

2. George Gilder, *Men and Marriage* (Gretna, La.: Pelican Publishing Co., 1986), p. 171.

Chapter 5

1. Warwick Williams, *Rekindling Desire: Bringing Your Sexual Relationship Back to Life* (Oakland, Calif.: New Harbinger, 1988), p. 109.
2. Bernie Zilbergeld, *The New Male Sexuality* (New York: Bantam, 1992), p. 67.

Chapter 8

1. Harold B. Smith, *Marriage Partnership*, Winter 1993, p. 48.
2. Harville Hendrix, *Getting the Love You Want* (New York: Harper & Row, 1990).
3. Neil Clark Warren, *Learning to Live with the Love of Your Life . . . and Loving It!* (Colorado Springs, Colo.: Focus on the Family, 1998).
4. Trent, et al., *Go the Distance: The Making of a Promise Keeper*, pp. 121-22.
5. John Gottman, *Why Marriages Succeed or Fail* (New York: Simon & Schuster, 1994).
6. Patricia Love, *Hot Monogamy* (New York: Penguin, 1995).

Chapter 12

1. *The Random House Dictionary of the English Language, the Unabridged Edition* (New York: Random House, 1967), p. 468.
2. Joseph C. Dillow, *Solomon on Sex* (Nashville: Thomas Nelson, 1977), p. 24.

The Gift of Sex (W Publishing Group, 2003)
A general handbook on sexuality for married couples of all stages
and ages

52 Ways to Have Fun, Fantastic Sex (Thomas Nelson, 1993)
One suggestion per week to add spark to married sex

Restoring the Pleasure (Word Publishing, 1993)
A complete self-help program to help couples overcome sexual
barriers

Getting Your Sex Life Off to a Great Start (Word Publishing, 1994)
A book to prepare engaged and newly married couples for a life
of exhilaration and mutual sex

Sex Facts for the Family (Word Publishing, 1992)
A reference book to help singles, couples, and parents with sexual
decisions and communication

The Magic and Mystery of Sex
Four video hours of Penner presentation and interviews of
couples bring new openness and joy to sex in marriage

Enjoying the Gift of Sex seminar
For information, visit our Web site or call.

If you can't find our products at your local bookstore, visit our Web site at *www.passionatecommitment.com.*

Or contact us at:

Dr. Clifford and Joyce Penner

200 East Del Mar Blvd., Suite 126

Pasadena, CA 91105

Phone: (626) 449-2525

Fax: (626) 564-1250

Clifford L. Penner is a clinical psychologist who holds a B.A. from Bethel College in St. Paul, Minnesota, an M.A. in theology from Fuller Theological Seminary, and a Ph.D. from Fuller's Graduate School of Psychology.

Joyce J. Penner is a clinical nurse specialist, with an emphasis on psychosomatic disorders, who holds a B.S. in nursing from the University of Washington and a master's degree in nursing from UCLA.

The Penners are recognized internationally as sex therapists, educators, and authors. In addition to their full-time sex therapy practice in Pasadena, California, and conducting sexual enhancement seminars, they have written *The Gift of Sex: A Couple's Guide to Sexual Fulfillment*; *Sex Facts for the Family: A Family Handbook on Sexuality*; *Restoring the Pleasure: Complete Step-by-Step Programs to Help Couples Overcome the Most Common Sexual Barriers*; *52 Ways to Have Fun, Fantastic Sex*; *Counseling for Sexual Disorders*; *What Every Wife Wants Her Husband to Know about Sex*; and *Getting Your Sex Life Off to a Great Start*. Joyce has also written *What to Pray When You're Expecting*.

FOCUS ON THE FAMILY®

Welcome to the family!

Whether you purchased this book, borrowed it, or received it as a gift, we're glad you're reading it. It's just one of the many helpful, encouraging, and biblically based resources produced by Focus on the Family for people in all stages of life.

Focus began in 1977 with the vision of one man, Dr. James Dobson, a licensed psychologist and author of numerous best-selling books on marriage, parenting, and family. Alarmed by the societal, political, and economic pressures that were threatening the existence of the American family, Dr. Dobson founded Focus on the Family with one employee and a once-a-week radio broadcast aired on 36 stations.

Now an international organization reaching millions of people daily, Focus on the Family is dedicated to preserving values and strengthening and encouraging families through the life-changing message of Jesus Christ.

Focus on the Family Magazines

These faith-building, character-developing publications address the interests, issues, concerns, and challenges faced by every member of your family from preschool through the senior years.

| Focus on the Family **Citizen®** U.S. news issues | Focus on the Family **Clubhouse Jr.™** Ages 4 to 8 | Focus on the Family **Clubhouse™** Ages 8 to 12 | **Breakaway®** Teen guys | **Brio®** Teen girls 12 to 16 | **Brio & Beyond®** Teen girls 16 to 19 | **Plugged In®** Reviews movies, music, TV |

More Great Resources
from Focus on the Family®

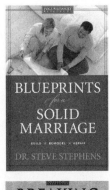

Blueprints for a Solid Marriage
By Dr. Steve Stephens
Marriage, like a house, requires time, effort, and regular maintenance. Whether you are building the foundation, making repairs, or needing to remodel your relationship, *Blueprints for a Solid Marriage* helps any time-strapped couple assess their relationship and then take action with an easy-to-follow plan and fun "marriage improvement projects." Hardcover

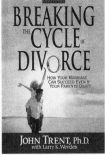

Breaking the Cycle of Divorce
by John Trent with Larry K. Weeden
When you come from a home of divorce, making your own marriage work can be tough. You can stop the cycle. In *Breaking the Cycle of Divorce,* psychologist and author John Trent—an adult child of divorce offers encouragement, insight and the tools to equip you to beat the odds. You can have a marriage that's strong and that gives your own children a solid foundation for a happily married life. Hardcover

Complete Guide to the First Five Years of Marriage: Launching a Lifelong, Successful Relationship
Thousands of couples have asked the counselors at Focus on the Family for insight into money, communication, and a host of other issues. Now their collective wisdom is available for you in this handy reference book. *Complete Guide to the First Five Years of Marriage.* Hardcover

FOR MORE INFORMATION

 Online:
Log on to www.family.org
In Canada, log on to www.focusonthefamily.ca.

 Phone:
Call toll free: (800) A-FAMILY
In Canada, call toll free: (800) 661-9800.

Focus
*on
the* Family®

BP06XP1